the New York Restaurant COOKBOOK

the New York Restaurant COOKBOOK

Recipes from the City's Best Chefs

FLORENCE FABRICANT

REVISED AND UPDATED EDITION

NYC
& Company
nycgo.com

RIZZOLI
NEW YORK

Revised and updatd edition published in the
United States of America in 2009
by Rizzoli International Publications, Inc.
300 Park Avenue South
New York, NY 10010
www.rizzoliusa.com
Originally published in 2003

2009 2010 2011 2012 2013 / 10 9 8 7 6 5 4 3 2 1

Printed in the United States of America

Designed by Patricia Fabricant

ISBN: 978-0-8478-3241-5

Library of Congress Control Number: 2008944133

THIS BOOK IS DEDICATED TO NEW YORK CITY'S
RESTAURANT COMMUNITY AND TO ALL
NEW YORKERS AND VISITORS WHO ENJOY
THE BEST OF DINING.

CONTENTS

PREFACE

GEORGE FERTITTA, CEO, NYC & COMPANY

Whether you call New York City home, are someone who loves to visit, or are simply a fan of superb food and restaurants, this book is for you. In addition to recipes from some of the city's most coveted kitchens, you'll also get a behind-the-scenes look at the unparalleled quality, impeccable hospitality, boundless energy, and distinct personality that characterize the New York City dining scene.

From landmark institutions to the latest hotspots, from world-renowned chefs to a diverse cross-section of ethnic eateries, New York City offers something for every taste, mood, and budget. This is a city where dining is truly celebrated and moments big and small happen around the table. It's where you can find the world's cuisines within a few blocks of each other and where the culture of dining lives—and thrives—in every neighborhood. Today, New York City offers the most varied and exciting dining experiences of any city in the world, with close to 19,000 licensed eating establishments, representing everything from corner delis to four-star culinary palaces.

Our restaurants always have their doors open to you and invite you to experience the quality, creativity, and vibrancy that have become synonymous with New York City dining. And now, we bring you more than 100 recipes that promise a taste of the city's most memorable meals right in your own kitchen. Also, by purchasing this book, you help support the NYC & Company Foundation, a charitable and educational organization whose mission is to support and promote New York City by encouraging tourism and the organizations that make visiting New York City a truly exceptional experience.

From our restaurants to your homes, let this book be your guide to the city's culinary culture. This is dining. This is New York City.™

FOREWORD

TRACY NIEPORENT

Many of life's most meaningful moments happen in restaurants, where you're dining with family, friends, and colleagues—sharing good conversation, and fine food and drink. For me, it started as a youngster, when our parents took my brother, Drew, and I out for dinner. We ate in a wide range of restaurants, with many different themes and cuisines. We tasted the foods of diverse cultures, and met chefs and restaurateurs who mesmerized our taste buds and taught us what hospitality was all about. The people we met had integrity and a great work ethic. In addition to these admirable qualities, they were working in an environment of creativity and theatricality. Who could ask for anything more?

One New York restaurant, in particular, caught my imagination. It was called Headquarters, and it was operated by Johnny Schwartz, chef to General Dwight D. Eisenhower during World War II. There were huge photographs of General and then President Eisenhower displayed all over the restaurant, together with images of other military and world leaders. The room had a larger-than-life quality, with flowing draperies on the ceiling, a seated balcony, and banquettes surrounding the large number of tables. Frank McGee, a prominent NBC newsman, often did live radio broadcasts and interviews from a corner table. There was always great people-watching, and a feeling that something big was about to happen. Our favorite moment came at dessert, which was always served on one's birthday with a sparkler blazing on top. Johnny always said to us, "If you can blow out the sparkler, you get to keep the restaurant." As hard as we blew, we could never blow the sparkler out. Yes, as it turns out, my brother and I have had to open every one of our restaurants the old-fashioned way—with lots of hard work.

In New York City, restaurants are an important part of our way of life. We've never had more great restaurants than right now. You can find any cuisine you crave here, and a range of prices that make dining accessible to virtually everyone. Since you're holding this cookbook, you're probably fond of our city's restaurants, and what you'll find in these pages is a labor of love. We hope you'll enjoy this opportunity to re-create what we put on the plate. We also look forward to serving you personally in our restaurants, so that we can demonstrate the quality, variety, and hospitality that make New York City the premiere dining destination in the world.

INTRODUCTION

FLORENCE FABRICANT

The kitchen has fascinated me, challenged me, and kept me entertained for almost as long as I can remember. And when I say "kitchen," I find it hard to separate my home kitchen from those in restaurants. New York's restaurant scene has had a profound influence on my life. Do I go out to dinner or light the stove? No contest for some people, but a dilemma for me.

It is not an overstatement to say that I first began tinkering with restaurant recipes when I was about four years old—but please do not imagine some prodigy whipping up Tournedos Rossini for the family instead of playing with blocks. My obsession then, as I still vividly recall, was adding just the right amount of soy sauce to my egg-drop soup until I was satisfied with the flavor and color. It did not matter whether the soup was made at the neighborhood chow mein palace or at Ruby Foo's—the original one—near Times Square.

My parents were avid restaurant-goers, and I was a lucky participant. I loved the glitter of fancy places. I remember my father taking me to Chambord on Third Avenue, which had all the different sizes of Champagne bottles in the window. I always insisted that he recite their names—jeroboam, Nebuchadnezzar, and so forth—before we went into the narrow storefront restaurant in the shadow of the "El."

My mother adored Forum of the Twelve Caesars and The Four Seasons. She did not like Dominick's and Mario's in the Bronx, but my father did; he took me to both and insisted that my mother prepare steaks for him the way they did, seasoned with garlic and olive oil. Before theater we would go to the Algonquin Hotel, where I liked the creamed chicken served under a glass bell, which the waiter removed with great ceremony. After theater, immense, crisply caramelized apple pancakes at Reuben's were a must. We would go to Rumpelmayer's on Central Park South for hot chocolate after skating in the Wollman Rink. Of course, I went to the Automat. And to the Tip-Toe Inn and the C&L when I visited friends on the Upper West Side. I remember these names better than those of some of my old boyfriends.

Although I was born in the Bronx, I grew up in Westchester County, and spent as much time as possible in Manhattan. In my early teens I attended classes at The Art Students League, and before taking the train home from Grand Central Terminal, I would always have a bowl of oyster stew at The Grand Central Oyster Bar. By myself.

Once, after eating the honey-soaked phyllo dessert called ekmek kadaif with kaymak at the Balkan-Armenian in the East Twenties, I asked the waiter to find out how it was made, especially the kaymak, a kind of dense clotted cream. The next day I spent an hour in the kitchen at home, cooking cream down and ladling it to aerate it as it condensed. The first gâteau Saint-Honoré I ever sampled, an indulgence of cream, caramel, custard, and crisp pastry, beckoned from a tall dessert cart at Voisin on Park Avenue. That one I did not attempt at home.

Far too few of the restaurant landmarks in the city's history and in my life before I was professionally involved in food linger as more than memories. There is a recipe for Oyster Stew from the Oyster Bar in this book, but I would have loved to include the sweetbreads with peas that I adored at Le Pavillon. I mourn Le Pavillon even as I celebrate the new stars that make New York's restaurant universe shine so brightly—Daniel, Jean Georges, Le Bernardin, and the others that fill many of the pages in this cookbook. The restaurants that have been included were selected in consultation with NYC & Company to represent all the boroughs and a cross-section of the city's ethnic fabric. And they are not limited just to high-profile places like Daniel and Jean Georges, or to the newest, hottest venues, but cover quite an array, from standbys like Sardi's and the Carnegie Deli to wd50 and its cutting-edge cooking on the newly gentrified Lower East Side. Williamsburg, Brooklyn, is represented by the hip Relish and the venerable Peter Luger Steak House.

For the first edition of this book, we worked to the last minute on the selection of the restaurants, as the scene was constantly evolving. Now, five years later, the pace of change is perhaps even faster, and the list of potential replacements has been rich and long. Though there is a growing trend toward multiple restaurant ownership by chefs and restaurateurs, we did not want to include more than one restaurant from any chef, restaurateur, or restaurant group, so some worthy newcomers were not added. And again, we were limited by the size and scope of the book. We also wanted to avoid duplicating restaurant styles and recipes. For this edition, we selected recipes similar to the ones that had to be replaced. And as before, they often had to be transformed and adapted for the home cook without violating the chef's intention.

Over my years as a food professional, I have spent enough time in restaurant kitchens to learn to deal with chefs' recipes and even to understand the shorthand in which many are written. I have acquired some good habits, like plucking the leaves of herbs off their stems, shocking blanched vegetables in ice water, taking time to reduce a sauce before bolstering it with a final dollop of butter, tossing drained pasta in the pan with the sauce and a bit of the pasta water instead of merely dumping the sauce on top, and tweezing out the pin bones from fish fillets. I have incorporated these techniques into the recipes. They will make you a better cook.

I am not antifat, and I use plenty of butter and oil in my own cooking. But I find that most chefs overdo it, or do not really measure when writing out their recipes, often estimating 6 tablespoons when 4 are enough. Also, the portion sizes in restaurants can be excessive at times. I adjusted the recipes accordingly.

I have also acquired an understanding of how much of a recipe can be done in advance, leaving only the final assembly to be done before serving. There is more tolerance than one might think. I have incorporated this advice into the recipes, too.

As demanding as it is to be a chef, in some respects they have it easier than home cooks. A chef would walk out the door if asked to prepare Marinated Hamachi with Green Apple Mustard and Cucumber Vinegar without the help of underlings to cut apples and cucumbers in precise little sticks and prepare croutons no bigger than pencil erasers. That recipe, from Alain Ducasse, is in the book; I wrestled it into submission, step by step. So are The Four Seasons' Crisp Farmhouse Duck, which has to be started four days in advance, and Mario Batali's delicious rabbit from Babbo, which requires disjointing and partly deboning two rabbits, making stock, peeling baby carrots, and shelling peas.

Unlike the home kitchen, restaurant kitchens have batches of stock, chopped onions, peeled garlic cloves, rinsed and dried lettuces, properly softened butter, and perfect sorbets at the ready, making everything from the prep work to the final assembly of a dish as efficient as possible. Home cooking is not like that. Except for some staples, every recipe requires a shopping list and more than one preparation task.

Because these recipes have come from restaurant kitchens, where the resources are not the same as in a home, some adjustments may be necessary when it comes to ingredients. For example, it is better to use well-flavored freshly made stocks instead of the canned variety or bouillon cubes. But a serious home cook is in luck. These days, many fancy food shops and online retailers sell high-quality veal, chicken, beef, lamb, and vegetable sauce bases and concentrates, which would be fine to use. The cucumber vinegar in the *hamachi* recipe is not an ingredient one finds on store shelves or even from online purveyors, which have become an increasingly valuable supplier. So I juiced a piece of cucumber in a garlic press and added it to some mild rice vinegar. And so can you!

Do make sure that your fresh ingredients are genuinely fresh and in good condition; the quality of these is not negotiable. It is better to substitute baby spinach for arugula if the latter looks wilted, or diced sea scallops for bay scallops if the latter have been frozen. Similarly, when you try the recipes in this book, there is no harm in making sensible substitutions like filet mignon for veal or for venison in order to guarantee the best results.

The freshness imperative also applies to spices and herbs. Many of the chefs have specified organic ingredients, but it is not essential that they be used. Some chefs also made a point of insisting on a particular variety of salt. In general, kosher or sea salt will be sufficient. And how much salt to use is a highly personal matter. Oils should be good quality: olive oil should always be extra virgin—those from Greece and Spain often represent the best value. The same holds true for vinegars; avoid supermarket balsamic. For most hard-to-find ethnic ingredients, I have listed reasonable substitutes.

Measuring is important. Chefs usually weigh ingredients instead of measuring them with cups and spoons. Although many of the ingredient amounts for these recipes have been given by volume, in many other books, weighing is essential. A good kitchen scale is a worthwhile investment.

There may be imprecision with timing. Not all stoves, ovens, and grills cook the same, and exactly 25 minutes in my oven might mean 20 or 35 in yours. It is important to learn to recognize when the ingredients have reached a certain stage of doneness—I have given guidelines to help with this.

Some of the dishes—such as the rabbit from Babbo—are demanding and involve serious kitchen time. Others, like City Hall's Delmonico Steak with blue cheese butter and Pearl Oyster Bar's Fried Cod Sandwich, are quite simple to prepare, and none requires unobtainable ingredients.

This is New York, after all, and there are very few components for a recipe that are not available somewhere. Butchers sell rabbits, although an advance order might be required. There are Korean supermarkets for sweet potato noodles and spice merchants who keep smoked paprika on hand. The days when a trip to Chinatown was necessary to buy fresh ginger are past. The list of resources in the back of the book will provide guidance for shopping—whether you live in New York or not, it's easy now to order ingredients by mail through many of the suppliers listed. And the Internet's many grocery sites, which include several maintained by some of the city's best purveyors, can also help.

These days chefs devise their dishes with a dozen different components. In adapting the recipes, I often simplified them. I omitted a few of the ingredients in Morimoto's black bean sauce because the original recipe yielded 3 cups but only a tablespoon of it was used to prepare the excellent halibut. The salad served with the Open-Face Tuna Salad Sandwich at Le Pain Quotidien was dropped, and I prepared Scarpetta's braised goat with boneless cubes of meat instead of starting with a whole shoulder and leg. Condiments like chutneys and even ketchup are often made in restaurant kitchens. Home cooks can substitute store-bought. Is there a dessert without an ice cream, a sauce or two, a delicate tuile, and a frivolous chocolate garnish? You are likely to find some of these adornments left off the plate, merely mentioned at the end of the recipe, or simplified. At Corton, the pear sorbet served alongside the pumpkin genoise is house-made, but I suggest that you purchase it instead.

Even the presentation of food in a restaurant is different from the way it is served at home. So instead of requiring that four or six portions each be plated separately, I give instructions for family-style service in bowls and on platters. August's classic Tarte Flambée appears as one large pastry to be cut into wedges, instead of as six or eight individual tartlets.

Incidentally, here is a restaurant tip: Before a plate goes onto a waiter's tray and into the dining room, someone with a clean cloth wipes any extraneous drips of sauce from the rim, something that can easily be done at home. And another one: Serve hot food on warm plates.

Wine suggestions made by the chef or the restaurant's wine director are included with each recipe. Sometimes they are fairly broad—"a Sauternes," for example—but in some instances they are more specific. The recommendations are meant only as guidelines.

The recipes provide an excellent cross-section of what dining in New York today has come to represent. Traditionalists will find Chicken Soup from the Second Avenue Deli, Caesar Salad from Tavern on the Green, Onion Soup Gratinée from Capsouto Frères, and a Bittersweet Chocolate Soufflé from Payard Bistro. Nostalgia buffs will not be able to pass on Patsy's Lobster Fra Diavolo, or André Soltner's chocolate mousse, added to this edition—but it is not from the shuttered Lutèce; the dessert is served by Tony Fortuna at his T-Bar Steak & Lounge. Those with the spirit of adventure may want to try Pampano's Lobster Tacos. For vegetarians, there is Hangawi's Vermicelli Genghis Khan. Cooks who cannot resist a challenge can set off into the wilds of the Ricotta and Spinach Dumplings from Felidia, the spiced seafood Yiouvesti stew from Anthos, the Goose Fat Potatoes from Strip House, or the Lemongrass-Crusted Swordfish with Thai Peanut Sauce from Roy's New York.

The cuisines range from American, both classic and contemporary, to Chinese, Indian, Thai, Vietnamese, Mexican, Greek, Italian, Italian-American, French, and Spanish. Steak-house specialties, brunch dishes, and cocktails are all in the book.

Trendy flavors like wasabi, luxury touches like a dollop of caviar or a slice of foie gras, and comfort food like deviled eggs and a version of macaroni and cheese are represented. The secret of Le Cirque's world-famous Crème Brûlée is revealed, as is how to make those omnipresent little molten chocolate cakes.

You might envy my family and many of our friends. We ate spectacularly well while I was testing the recipes. But now that the book is done, I return to the big question, my perennial dilemma: Do I go out to dinner or into the kitchen tonight?

APPETIZERS

GOUGÈRES 18

ZUCCHINI CARPACCIO 21

CRACKLING CALAMARI SALAD WITH LIME-MISO DRESSING 22

MARINATED HAMACHI WITH GREEN APPLE MUSTARD
AND CUCUMBER VINEGAR 24

TORO TARTARE 27

MUSSEL SALAD WITH ARTICHOKES AND HARICOTS VERTS 28

GREEN ASPARAGUS WITH MORELS AND ASPARAGUS SAUCE 30

LEEKS BRAISED IN RED WINE 32

MOULES MARINIÈRES 33

YACHE PAJUN, VEGETABLE SCALLION PANCAKE 34

LITTLENECK CLAMS CASINO 36

LOBSTER CAKES WITH CUCUMBER-GINGER SALAD 38

LOBSTER TACOS 40

FONDUTA 43

TOMATO TATIN 44

SEARED FOIE GRAS WITH ASIAN PEAR–ENDIVE SALAD 46

GOUGÈRES

ARTISANAL

> *It's ironic that Artisanal,* a brasserie-style restaurant, occupies what once was the New York version of La Coupole, the famous Parisian brasserie. Between incarnations the space had a highly regarded run as An American Place. Now, as Artisanal, it features an enormous Belle Époque painting from a French railway station on one wall and, because the restaurant's emphasis is on cheese, a retail counter along another. Terrance Brennan, the chef and owner, has had a long love affair with cheese. His Lincoln Center–area restaurant, Picholine, is known for its outstanding selection. Brennan has also opened a wholesale cheese center where cheeses are aged and distributed, and where classes and receptions are held.

MAKES 36 PIECES

¾ cup all-purpose flour
¼ teaspoon baking powder
4 tablespoons unsalted butter
¼ cup plus 2 tablespoons milk
1¼ teaspoons sea salt
6 grinds black pepper
3 eggs, at room temperature
1 cup coarsely grated Gruyère
   cheese

Preheat the oven to 375 degrees. Line 2 baking sheets with parchment. Sift the flour and baking powder together and set aside.

Put the butter, ¼ cup of the milk, ¼ teaspoon of the salt, the pepper, and ½ cup of water in a 2-quart saucepan. Set over medium heat, bring to a boil, and cook until the butter melts, then remove from the heat. Dump in the flour mixture all at once, stir well with a wooden spoon, and return to the heat. Cook gently for a minute or two, stirring until the mixture starts to pull away from the sides of the saucepan and forms a ball. Transfer the dough to an electric mixer with a paddle attachment and beat at low speed until the mixture is just warm. You can do this by hand, but it's a tough job. A food processor, however, is also effective.

Add the eggs one at a time, beating to incorporate after each addition. Add ½ cup of the cheese. Beat until the mixture is smooth and shiny, about 10 minutes.

These gougères are lightened by the long beating and the addition of baking powder.

Though Gruyère is the classic cheese, other varieties, including Parmigiano-Reggiano, Roquefort, or even Cheddar, can be used.

A tablespoon or two of minced herbs can also be added just before the end of beating.

Gougères can be made in advance and frozen, then briefly reheated in a 350-degree oven, 10 to 15 minutes.

Using a pastry bag or 2 teaspoons, form 1-inch mounds on a baking sheet, placing them about an inch apart. You should be able to fit 18 gougères on a baking sheet. Gently brush the tops of the gougères with the remaining milk, and sprinkle each with a generous pinch of the remaining cheese and salt. Bake until puffed and deep gold, about 20 to 25 minutes. Remove from baking sheet and serve while still warm.

Champagne, or a white or red wine from Burgundy

ZUCCHINI CARPACCIO

> *Fig & Olive began in modest fashion,* as a bright little restaurant with several dining counters and tables, on the Upper East Side. A retail area where customers could purchase the fine olive oils that the restaurant used in its cooking was an important part of the design. It expanded into grander premises in the meat-packing district, and then into a third restaurant in midtown. Olive branches, pots of fresh herbs, and simple, fragrant, Mediterranean cooking have been its formula from the beginning. This zucchini carpaccio clearly demonstrates that philosophy.

SERVES 6 TO 8

1 pound medium-small zucchini, sliced paper-thin

¼ cup extra virgin olive oil

Juice of 1 lemon

Salt and freshly ground black pepper

6 tablespoons shaved Parmigiano Reggiano

4 tablespoons toasted pine nuts

A delicate white with citrus notes like a vermentino from Provence.

Arrange the zucchini slices, slightly overlapping, on a large, flat platter. Cover with plastic wrap. Refrigerate until ready to serve.

In a small bowl whisk the olive oil and lemon juice together.

Just before serving, whisk the olive oil dressing briefly to blend it, drizzle it over the zucchini, season with salt and pepper, scatter the cheese and the pine nuts on top, and serve.

Unless you are highly skilled at knife work, it's best to use a mandoline to slice the zucchini.

The best tool for shaving the cheese is an ordinary vegetable peeler.

The carpaccio can be arranged on individual plates instead of on a single platter.

CRACKLING CALAMARI SALAD WITH LIME-MISO DRESSING

CHINA GRILL

China Grill is the flagship of an ever-expanding restaurant group owned by Jeffrey Chodorow. Represented in Manhattan by the original China Grill, Kobe Club, Asia de Cuba, and Center Cut, it also has a strong foothold in Miami, San Francisco, Las Vegas, Los Angeles, London, and Mexico City. China Grill, with quotations from Marco Polo's writings embedded in the floor, was one of New York's first Pacific Rim restaurants. This calamari salad, which combines Japanese, Thai, and Italian influences, is a fine example.

SERVES 4

1 tablespoon chopped fresh ginger

1 large garlic clove

2 tablespoons soy sauce

¼ cup mellow white miso paste

¼ cup rice vinegar

¼ cup lime juice

6½ cups soybean oil

1 head radicchio, cored and sliced very thin

1 head frisée, cored and sliced thin

½ cup cornstarch, sifted

10 ounces cleaned squid (calamari), sliced in thin rings, plus the tentacles

Sea salt

To make the dressing: turn on the food processor and drop the ginger and garlic through the feed tube. Process until they are minced. Stop the machine and scrape down the sides. Add the soy sauce, miso, vinegar, and lime juice. Whirl briefly to blend. With the machine running, slowly add ½ cup of the soybean oil, just as though making mayonnaise. Process until the dressing is emulsified, then transfer it to a container with a pouring spout. You should have about 1½ cups of dressing.

Toss the radicchio and frisée together in a bowl, then toss again with half the dressing. Spread it on a rimmed platter.

Heat the remaining 6 cups of oil in a wok or a large, deep saucepan to 360 degrees. Set a large bowl near the stove and line it with paper towels. Place the cornstarch in a bowl, add the calamari rings and tentacles, and toss with your fingers until they are well-coated. When the oil reaches 360 degrees, drop in the calamari. Use a wooden fork or a pair of chopsticks to separate the rings as much as you can, and swirl the oil gently as the calamari cooks. When the calamari is golden—and this will take a good 5 to 8 minutes, longer than you might think—scoop it out

Most fried calamari is dusted with flour. This recipe, using cornstarch instead, results in lighter squid rings that stay crisp longer, even when doused with dressing.

with a skimmer or a slotted spoon, place it in the paper-lined bowl and sprinkle it with sea salt. Pull out the paper towel, distributing the salt, then spread the calamari on the salad. Drizzle with the remaining dressing and serve.

Pinot noir or sauvignon blanc

MARINATED HAMACHI WITH GREEN APPLE MUSTARD AND CUCUMBER VINEGAR

ADOUR BY ALAIN DUCASSE

Ducasse, a multistarred French chef, closed his restaurant in the Essex House in early 2008 and within the year, opened this gracious and stunning new place in what had been Lespinasse in the St. Regis hotel. David Rockwell's design respects the structure and fine architectural details of the room while giving it gilded warmth. The name is that of a river flowing through Ducasse's hometown in southwestern France. The restaurant has a decided wine component and one of the most reasonable and eclectic lists in the city. The cooking is also somewhat eclectic, though clearly rooted in France.

1 slice stale white sandwich bread

2 tablespoons clarified butter

1 pound *hamachi* (yellowtail),
 wild Pacific salmon, or arctic
 char fillet

½ English cucumber, peeled

2 tablespoons rice vinegar

2½ tablespoons extra virgin olive oil

1 Granny Smith apple, peeled
 and cored

1 tablespoon Dijon mustard

Salt and freshly ground black pepper

Remove the crusts from the bread and cut the slice into tiny cubes. Heat the butter in a small pan, add the bread, and sauté it until it is golden. Set it aside.

Slice the fish on the bias, scarcely ¼ inch thick, and arrange the slices on each of 4 plates. Cover and refrigerate.

Cut a slice ½ inch thick from the cucumber, force it through a garlic press, and mix the juice with 1½ tablespoons of the vinegar and 2 tablespoons of the olive oil. Set aside. Cut the rest of the cucumber in julienne matchsticks about 1½ inches long.

Crush one-eighth of the apple in a mortar, force it through a strainer, and mix the juice with the mustard. Whisk in the remaining ½ tablespoon of the oil. Cut the rest of the apple in julienne matchsticks about 1½ inches long and toss with the remaining ½ tablespoon vinegar.

To serve, remove the fish from the refrigerator. Drizzle each portion with some of the cucumber dressing and dust with salt and pepper. Arrange the cucumber and apple sticks on either side of the fish and trace with the apple-mustard dressing. Scatter the little croutons over the fish. Serve.

A crisp white falanghina from Campania, Italy, or a chenin blanc demi-sec from the Loire Valley. These choices highlight the range of wine director Thomas Combescot's list.

Hamachi, or yellowtail, is a Pacific fish popular among chefs and at sushi bars. It is pale and pristine and is not a kind of tuna (that's yellowfin). But few retail fish markets sell it, though there are some online sources that carry a farmed variety. If you cannot find it, wild Pacific salmon, especially king salmon, can be used, as can arctic char, which is more delicate.

The original recipe calls for cucumber vinegar and green apple mustard to season the fish and the apple-cucumber garnish. These ingredients may be fairly ordinary for chefs who have astonishing resources, but for home cooks, it's another matter. This recipe offers makeshift but effective solutions: cucumber juice mixed with Japanese rice vinegar, and apple combined with everyday Dijon mustard.

TORO TARTARE

JEWEL BAKO

Jewel is the operative term for this tiny Japanese restaurant, which may be the most elegant spot in the still-funky East Village. Jack Lamb, a former maître d'hôtel at Bouley, and his wife, Grace, do not compromise on ingredients or presentation for pricey *kaiseki*, or set dinners. A sushi bar in the rear, beyond the arched wooden ceiling of the main room, has a few seats for those who prefer to pick and choose. The Lambs have also opened Degustation, a tasting bar next door; and Jack's Luxury Oyster Bar around the corner.

SERVES 4

2 tablespoons drained capers
2 tablespoons extra virgin olive oil
2 tablespoons grated fresh ginger
Sea salt
12 ounces sushi-quality tuna
½ ripe Hass avocado, peeled
2 teaspoons lime juice
2 teaspoons soy sauce
½ teaspoon prepared wasabi paste
1 ounce osetra caviar

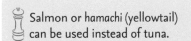
Salmon or hamachi (yellowtail) can be used instead of tuna.

In a mortar, crush the capers, work in the olive oil, and finally the ginger. Season the mixture with a pinch of sea salt. Finely dice the tuna and fold it into the caper mixture. Do not combine the tuna and the seasoning more than 20 minutes before serving.

Mash the avocado, mixing in the lime juice as you go. Mix in the soy sauce and wasabi, adjusting the amounts to taste.

To serve, pack the tuna so it nearly fills a half-cup metal measuring cup and turn it out onto a small salad plate. Repeat with the remaining tuna on 3 more plates. Spread the avocado mixture on top of each serving of tuna and top with the caviar.

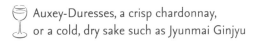
Auxey-Duresses, a crisp chardonnay, or a cold, dry sake such as Jyunmai Ginjyu

MUSSEL SALAD WITH ARTICHOKES AND HARICOTS VERTS

OUEST

Tom Valenti put to rest the conventional wisdom that there is no room for a fine restaurant on the Upper West Side beyond the Lincoln Center area. After he opened Ouest, a number of other chefs followed suit, so that now the Upper West Side offers more than sushi bars, Tex-Mex joints, and pizza. Valenti's career has taken him to many parts of the city, but he is right at home in his open kitchen on Upper Broadway, producing big flavors for the local regulars and for those who would venture to this part of the city for a meal, not just to shop at Zabar's. His second restaurant, West Branch, is nearby.

Do not be daunted by the process of removing all the leaves and the choke from the artichokes and throwing this debris away. The fleshy heart, sometimes called the bottom, is the best part of the vegetable.

See page 65 for directions on making homemade mayonnaise, but omit the anchovies and cheese.

Big green-lipped mussels from New Zealand are excellent to use.

New Zealand sauvignon blanc from the Marlborough region

SERVES 6

6 globe artichokes

Juice of 1 lemon

1 cup dry white wine

4 garlic cloves, peeled and smashed

2 pounds mussels, scrubbed and debearded (see tip, page 33)

⅔ cup mayonnaise, preferably homemade (see tip)

1 generous tablespoon Dijon mustard

2 tablespoons minced shallots

Pinch cayenne

Salt and freshly ground black pepper

6 ounces *haricots verts* or fresh green beans, trimmed and cut in thirds

3 tablespoons extra virgin olive oil

6 small bunches mâche or 3 cups fresh watercress leaves

Preparing this salad is a multi-step procedure, but once all the components are ready, the assembly becomes a snap. First, trim all the leaves from the artichokes. Use a paring knife to trim away the fuzzy choke, taking care not to cut away the fleshy heart. Neatly trim off the stem and the edges around the heart. Place the hearts in a bowl, add half of the lemon juice plus water to cover, and set aside.

Heat the wine and garlic in a 3-quart saucepan. Add the mussels, cover, and simmer until the mussels open, about 6 minutes. Remove the mussels, leaving any unopened ones in the pan. Steam these for another 2 minutes, then discard any that still have not opened. Remove the mussels from the shells and place the mussels in a bowl. Discard the shells. Strain the mussel cooking liquid and reserve 3 tablespoons.

Beat together the mayonnaise, mustard, reserved mussel broth, shallots, cayenne, and salt and pepper to taste. Fold half this dressing into the mussels. Set aside in the refrigerator.

Bring a 2-quart pot of salted water to a boil. Cook the artichoke hearts until tender, about 10 minutes; remove them with a slotted spoon and set aside. Add the *haricots verts* to the boiling water and blanch for 1 minute. Drain and place in a bowl of ice water. When the beans are cool, dry them on paper towels, then transfer to a large bowl and toss with 1 tablespoon of the olive oil. Add the mâche and the remaining oil and lemon juice to the bowl and toss again.

Slice the artichoke hearts vertically, about ¼ inch thick, and arrange slices in a circle on 6 salad plates. Pile some of the mussels in the center of the artichoke hearts. Make a mound of the mâche and *haricots verts* salad on top of each, drizzle the remaining mayonnaise dressing over and around the salad, and serve.

GREEN ASPARAGUS WITH MORELS AND ASPARAGUS SAUCE

JEAN GEORGES

> *Some New Yorkers* wonder whether Jean-Georges Vongerichten has an identical twin. Although he is the chef and partner in five restaurants in the city and several others around the world, with more on the way, he seems almost always to be in the gleaming open kitchen at his flagship restaurant, Jean Georges. He's an inventive cook, one who soaks up new ideas like a sponge and creates food that is original, thought-provoking, and filled with flavor. His tightly wound personality translates into restaurants that inspire passion with every bite.

SERVES 6

1 bunch pencil asparagus, woody ends snapped off

2 tablespoons unsalted butter

3 tablespoons *vin jaune* or oloroso sherry

Salt and freshly ground white pepper

1 shallot, peeled and diced

½ pound fresh morels, rinsed well and dried

2 tablespoons heavy cream

36 jumbo asparagus, ends snapped off and peeled

> Vin jaune, a golden wine from the Jura region of France, has become extremely popular with chefs (see also page 51). The best vin jaune is Château-Chalon. The wine has a sherry-like quality.
>
> Morels can harbor sand in their deeply pitted surfaces. Rinse them well and allow them to dry.

Cut the pencil asparagus into 1-inch lengths. Place them in a saucepan with water to cover and boil a couple of minutes until tender. Drain, reserving ½ cup of the cooking water. Puree the asparagus in a blender, adding some of the cooking water to thin the mixture. Strain through a fine sieve into a small saucepan and heat gently over low heat. Whisk in 1 tablespoon of the butter, 2 tablespoons of the *vin jaune* or sherry, and salt and pepper to taste. Remove from the heat and set aside, covered.

Melt the remaining tablespoon of butter in a 10-inch skillet over low heat. Add the shallot and cook until softened. Increase the heat to medium, add the morels, and sauté until the morels are fully cooked, about 10 minutes. Stir in the remaining *vin jaune* and the cream. Simmer a few minutes until thickened. Season with salt and pepper, and set aside.

Cook the jumbo asparagus in a large pot of salted boiling water about 6 minutes, until tender, then drain. Arrange 6 of the spears side by side on each plate. Reheat the asparagus sauce and spoon it along one side of the plate. Reheat the morels and spoon them along the opposite side of the plate.

 A northern Italian white from Friuli

LEEKS BRAISED IN RED WINE

BALDORIA

This two-story spot in the theater district is the offspring of what is probably New York's most exclusive restaurant—Rao's, an East Harlem bar-restaurant that does not accept reservations from persons unknown to the management. Regulars have their tables, but others who have some insider connection can sometimes secure a spot that's not being used by its "owner." Frank Jr., son of Frank Pellegrino, an owner of Rao's, decided he wanted to strike out on his own, so with his father's blessing, he opened Baldoria. Some of the Italian-American specialties for which Rao's is known, such as baked clams, meatballs, and lemon chicken, are on Baldoria's menu, but more ambitious food is also offered in the casual, tiled-floor setting.

SERVES 4 TO 6

12 slender leeks (about 2 pounds), well-trimmed, with about 2 inches of green

1 tablespoon unsalted butter

⅓ cup dry red wine

½ cup veal stock

Salt and freshly ground black pepper

1 tablespoon balsamic vinegar

1 tablespoon minced flat-leaf parsley leaves

Use a sharp knife to quarter the tops of the leeks vertically through the green and to where the white begins. Rinse thoroughly and pat dry.

Melt the butter in a large, heavy sauté pan. Add the leeks, roll in the butter, cover, and cook a few minutes until they begin to sweat. Add the wine, veal stock, and salt and pepper. Cover and braise until tender, about 10 minutes. Baste the leeks with the vinegar, then lift them out of the pan, drain them well, and arrange on a serving platter.

Cook the remaining liquid over high heat until reduced to about ½ cup. Season to taste, then pour over the leeks, scatter the parsley on top and serve hot or at room temperature.

Rutherford Hill Merlot 2000 or another California merlot, or Rosso di Montalcino Collemattoni 2000

Leeks are often sold in uneven 1-pound bunches, with both thick and thin stalks. For this recipe, it's best to buy loose leeks, so you can select uniformly slender ones.

MOULES MARINIÈRES

Few of New York's restaurants evoke Belle Époque France as beautifully as L'Absinthe. The setting, with its globe lights, intricate tile floors, posters, mirrors, and brass trim, suggests the ultimate neighborhood bistro or brasserie. But it is not just a pretty face. The chef and owner, Jean-Michel Bergougnoux, has the finest credentials and offers a menu that covers both traditional dishes, like moules marinières, and more original fare. Perhaps it's the setting, for at L'Absinthe's comfortable banquettes, the classics are what whet the appetite.

SERVES 4

6 pounds mussels, preferably Prince Edward Island

2 tablespoons extra virgin olive oil

2 tablespoons unsalted butter

4 shallots, peeled and finely chopped

1 bouquet garni (a few parsley sprigs, thyme sprigs, and a bay leaf tied together)

1½ cups dry white wine

Freshly ground white pepper

Crusty baguette or country bread

Muscadet sur Lie, the most recent vintage

In addition to removing the "beard," or byssus, by pulling it off with a knife, a chef will take care to trim off the bit of gray filament along the edge of the mussel.

Scrub mussels and debeard as necessary.

Place a small stockpot over medium heat. Add the oil and butter, stir in the shallots, and cook until the shallots are translucent, about 2 minutes. Add the bouquet garni, mussels, and wine. Turn heat to high. When the wine simmers, reduce heat to medium, cover, and cook until mussels open, about 6 minutes. Discard any that do not open. Transfer mussels to 4 soup plates. Season the broth with pepper to taste, spoon over mussels, being careful not to scoop any sandy residue from the bottom of the pot, and serve, with crusty bread on the side.

YACHE PAJUN, VEGETABLE SCALLION PANCAKE

DO HWA

Growing up in Queens, Jenny Kwak and her sisters were privileged to enjoy their mother's excellent Korean home cooking. To give New Yorkers an idea of just how good Korean food could be, Kwak opened Dok Suni's, in the East Village, using her family's recipes and enlisting her mother to supervise the cooks. A friendly spot that did not seek a Korean clientele like the restaurants in "Little Korea" on West 32nd Street, Dok Suni's was so successful that the mother-daughter team opened Do Hwa, a more sophisiticated venue in Greenwich Village.

2 teaspoons soy sauce

½ teaspoon red pepper flakes

1 teaspoon sesame seeds

⅓ cup rice vinegar

2 medium-size zucchini (about 10 ounces)

1 bunch scallions, trimmed

4 *shiso* leaves, sold in Asian markets (also called beefsteak plant or *perilla)*

1 cup all-purpose flour

¾ teaspoon salt

1 egg

½ teaspoon *dashida* (Korean beef stock base), or beef bouillon powder, optional

¼ cup peanut oil

Unlike most recipes, this one doesn't call for preheating the pan before adding the batter. That's so the vegetables have time to cook before the batter has browned.

This is a last-minute dish: fried, cut in pieces, and served at once. But the various components of the pancake can be readied and the sauce assembled in advance. First, combine the soy sauce, pepper flakes, sesame seeds, and vinegar in a small bowl. This is the dipping sauce. Set aside.

Using a paring knife, slice off wide strips of the zucchini skin, leaving only ⅛ inch of the flesh attached. Julienne the strips lengthwise, then cut them into 1-inch pieces. Discard the rest of the zucchini—it contains too much water for the recipe. Cut the scallions in half lengthwise, then on an angle into 1-inch pieces. Roll the *shiso* leaves and slice them into thin shreds.

When you're ready to cook the pancake, whisk the flour and salt in a large mixing bowl. Beat the egg, ¾ cup cold water, and the beef stock base if using. Whisk the egg mixture into the flour mixture to make a batter. Fold in the zucchini strips, scallions, and *shiso*. Allow to rest 2 minutes so the batter can begin to soften the vegetables.

Pour the oil into a 10- or 12-inch skillet. Nonstick isn't necessary, but it helps. Add the batter to the cold skillet. Turn the heat to medium-high and cook the pancake until it's golden on the bottom. Run a spatula around the edge of the pancake to loosen it, place a large plate over the skillet, flip, then slide the pancake back into the skillet to cook the other side. Remove the pancake to the paper towels to drain it briefly. Cut it into wedges and serve with the dipping sauce.

 Korean or other Asian beer, or the mild Korean sweet potato vodka called soju

LITTLENECK CLAMS CASINO

PORTER HOUSE NEW YORK

Michael Lomonaco, one of New York's most beloved chefs, went from near despair after the destruction of Windows on the World on September 11, 2001, to renewed hope with this surefire success of a steak house in the Time Warner Center at Columbus Circle. It did not happen overnight, but when it did, Lomonaco knew it was right. The menu leaves enough opportunity for a creative chef. These crowd-pleasing clams are one of the most popular dishes. They are served as an appetizer in the sprawling main dining room and as a piquant accompaniment to drinks in the comfortable bar area.

8 ounces pancetta, finely diced

½ cup minced red bell pepper

½ cup minced yellow bell pepper

½ cup minced onion

1½ sticks (12 tablespoons) soft unsalted butter

2 tablespoons lemon juice

4 tablespoons finely minced flat-leaf parsley leaves

1 teaspoon smoked paprika

Salt and freshly ground pepper

36 littleneck clams, opened, on the half-shell

½ cup fine dry bread crumbs

2 tablespoons freshly grated Parmigiano Reggiano

½ teaspoon dried oregano

¼ cup extra virgin olive oil

Lemon wedges, for serving

Crusty bread, for serving

Smoked paprika is a Spanish specialty. Good-quality Hungarian sweet paprika can be used instead.

The special pans used to make French madeleine cookies are great for baking clams. Cover them with foil and put a clam in each cookie mold.

In a large skillet cook the pancetta over medium heat until it releases some of its fat, about 5 minutes. Remove it, drain it well on paper towels, and set it aside. Place the bell peppers and onion in the skillet and cook them together over medium heat until soft, about 5 minutes. Remove and reserve them.

In a bowl combine the butter, bell peppers and onion, pancetta, lemon juice, 3 tablespoons of the parsley, and the paprika and mix well. Season with salt and pepper. Place the clams on a baking sheet lined with crumpled aluminum foil to hold them steady. Place a teaspoon of the butter mixture on each clam.

In a separate bowl mix the bread crumbs, cheese, and oregano. Season with pepper. Sprinkle the crumbs evenly over the clams and drizzle the olive oil on top. Refrigerate until just before you are ready to serve.

To finish the dish, preheat the oven to 450 degrees. Bake the clams until the bread crumbs are golden brown, about 8 minutes. Sprinkle the remaining parsley leaves on top and serve immediately, with lemon wedges and crusty bread for sopping up the savory juices.

A bracing, citric albariño, preferably from California, not Spain.

LOBSTER CAKES WITH CUCUMBER-GINGER SALAD

'21' CLUB

The name of the restaurant refers to the address—21 West 52nd Street—and "club" is a holdover from the days when the premises housed a speakeasy. '21' was founded in 1930, during Prohibition, and in fact, its former wine cellar, now a private dining room, is still reached through a hidden door. The wine collection at '21' even included some so-called "medicinal" wines in an attempt to circumvent the Volstead Act. Today, the double town house, with its wrought-iron balustrades and painted jockeys standing at attention, still attracts regulars to its dining room, where the tables are covered with red-checked cloths and the ceiling is hung with toys and souvenirs. And classic old standbys on the menu such as the '21' Burger and the Chicken Hash are still favorites.

SERVES 4

6 tablespoons extra virgin olive oil

½ jalapeño chile, seeded and minced

½ cup minced, seeded red bell pepper

½ cup minced onion

Salt and freshly ground white pepper

2 egg yolks

1 tablespoon Tabasco

2 tablespoons lime juice

5 tablespoons mayonnaise

2 tablespoons Dijon mustard

1 tablespoon minced chives

½ tablespoon minced flat-leaf parsley

2 teaspoons minced cilantro leaves

Heat 2 tablespoons of the oil in a sauté pan. Add the jalapeño, red bell pepper, and onion. Season with salt and pepper. Sauté over low heat, until the vegetables are soft but not brown. Remove the vegetables to a bowl and set aside to cool about 30 minutes.

In a large mixing bowl, combine egg yolks, Tabasco, and lime juice. Lightly blend in the mayonnaise, mustard, chives, parsley, cilantro, and cayenne. Fold in the lobster, reserved sautéed vegetables, soft bread crumbs, and ¼ cup of the panko. Spread the remaining panko evenly on a pan at least 8 by 8 inches. Pack one-quarter of the lobster mixture into an empty 6-ounce tuna fish can (or a ramekin) and place the can, open side down, onto the panko. Lift off the can. Repeat with the remaining lobster mixture. Sprinkle the extra panko from the pan onto the tops of the cakes, pressing a tablespoon or more of the panko onto each cake. Refrigerate for at least 30 minutes.

Pinch cayenne

½ pound fresh cooked lobster meat cut into ½-inch pieces (see tip)

½ cup soft fresh bread crumbs

1¼ cups *panko* (Japanese white bread crumbs)

1 tablespoon unsalted butter

Cucumber-Ginger Salad (recipe follows)

2 medium cucumbers, peeled, halved lengthwise, seeded, and sliced thin

⅓ cup Japanese pickled ginger, coarsely chopped

3 tablespoons juice from pickled ginger

3 tablespoons rice vinegar

2 tablespoons minced dill leaves

Freshly ground white pepper

Alsatian gewürztraminer, full of fruit

You can buy cooked, shelled lobster meat, or you can boil a 1¾-pounder in a large pot of water for about 8 minutes, and you'll have your ½ pound of lobster meat. Two 1-pound lobsters, which cost less, can also be used; boil them for about 6 minutes.

Preheat the oven to 400 degrees. Heat the remaining 4 tablespoons of oil in a large ovenproof skillet. Place the lobster cakes in the skillet and sauté over medium heat until golden brown on the bottom. Carefully turn the cakes, add the butter to skillet, cook 1 minute, and transfer the pan to the oven. Bake until golden brown, about 4 minutes. Using a spatula, transfer the cakes to individual plates, place some of the Cucumber-Ginger Salad alongside, and serve.

CUCUMBER-GINGER SALAD

Place cucumbers in a bowl. Add the ginger, ginger juice, and vinegar. Mix well. Fold in dill. Season with pepper.

LOBSTER TACOS

PAMPANO

What is it about celebrity restaurants in New York? Sports figures sometimes do well, though most of the time, their places are branches of nationwide franchises. But Marla Maples and Britney Spears could not survive as restaurateurs. Only when the celebrity is discreetly in the background, the way Robert De Niro operates, does it seem to work. Placido Domingo had a hard time fulfilling his restaurant dream with his name on the marquee. First he tried Spanish food, then a blend of Spanish and Mexican. Now, lightened and brightened, and with his presence strictly behind the scenes, the restaurant has become Pampano, specializing in Mexican seafood.

2 live lobsters, each 1½ pounds

1½ tablespoons unsalted butter

1 tablespoon extra virgin olive oil

½ cup finely chopped onion

2 garlic cloves, minced

2 *chiles de arból*, or ½ teaspoon
  red pepper flakes

2 tablespoons tomato paste

1 cup heavy cream

¼ cup chicken stock

Salt

3 tablespoons minced cilantro leaves

½ cup canned black beans, rinsed
  and drained

4 flour tortillas

1 ripe Hass avocado, peeled and
  sliced

If you prefer, you can purchase 1 pound of cooked lobster meat for this recipe.

A rich California white, preferably a blend, or a chardonnay from Napa

There are four separate components to this recipe, each of which needs to be prepared before the tacos can be assembled and served. But all can be done in advance and reheated at the last minute.

Boil the lobsters for about 6 minutes. Drain and set aside. When they're cool enough to handle, crack the shells and extract the meat. Dice the meat into ½-inch pieces and place it in a small pan with the butter, covered.

For the sauce, heat the oil in a medium saucepan, add the onion, garlic, and chiles, and gently sauté until the onion is translucent. Stir in the tomato paste, cook for a moment, then stir in the cream. Cook about 5 minutes until thickened; stir in the chicken stock, season with salt and add 1 tablespoon of the cilantro. Set aside.

Puree or finely mash the black beans, adding enough water to make a mixture about the consistency of sour cream.

Just before serving, strain the cream sauce and gently reheat it; keep warm. Reheat the lobster with the butter and keep warm. Heat the beans. Place over high heat a griddle or a cast-iron skillet large enough to hold a tortilla. Add one tortilla, heat for 45 seconds, until the tortilla starts to blister, turn and heat another 15 seconds. Remove the tortilla to a flat surface. Spread one-quarter of the black beans in a line down the center, top with one-quarter of the lobster, spoon on about 3 generous tablespoons of the sauce, add about 4 slices of the avocado, and sprinkle with ½ tablespoon of the cilantro. Roll the tortilla around the filling and place it, seam side down, on a warm serving platter. Repeat with the remaining tortillas and serve at once.

FONDUTA

Sebastiano Maioglio opened his restaurant, Barbetta, in 1906 in twin brownstone Astor town houses that were built in 1874 and 1881. The restaurant is now owned and run by his daughter, Laura Maioglio. Embellished with crystal chandeliers and fine woodwork, Barbetta also has one of the city's most elegant gardens for outdoor dining on soft summer evenings. It has always specialized in the cooking of the Piedmont region of northern Italy. Fonduta, a simple cheese appetizer that can be ennobled with shavings of white truffle, is a classic of the region. Laura Maioglio serves the fonduta in a nest of crisply cooked Parmigiano-Reggiano and decorates it with whole quail eggs, for a unique dish that has to be prepared one serving at a time. At home, a simple fonduta with a scattering of fresh white truffles in season will do just fine.

SERVES 4

1 (12-inch) baguette, sliced thin

½ cup milk

6 ounces Italian Fontina Val d'Aosta cheese, rind removed, diced

2 egg yolks

1 (1-ounce) fresh white truffle or 2 teaspoons white truffle oil (sold in fancy food shops), optional

If you use white truffle oil, be sure that it's fresh and of good quality. Always store it in the refrigerator. It can be omitted.

This recipe calls for some fast action. Everything has to be ready to serve as soon as it is finished. So get your crostini ready first. Lightly toast the baguette slices and arrange them on a platter around a shallow 12- ounce ceramic bowl.

Place a heavy 2-quart saucepan over low heat, add the milk, and when it begins to warm, add the cheese. Stir with a whisk. When the cheese and milk are smooth and creamy, add the egg yolks, and beat them vigorously into the cheese mixture. As soon as the yolks are incorporated, remove the pan from the heat. Beat for another minute, then pour the fonduta into the waiting bowl.

If you have a fresh truffle, wait until you present the fonduta at the table before shaving it on top to maximize the aroma. Otherwise, drizzle the white truffle oil on the fonduta right before seving. Guests can dip the crostini into the cheese mixture.

Sparkling white Prosecco from the Piedmont region of Italy

TOMATO TATIN

Take the Tarte Tatin formula, an upside-down apple tart, and turn it into a savory dish and you have this version, bursting with ripe, seasonal tomatoes on a puff-pastry base. The restaurant, La Goulue, is also based on a formula, that of the many Art Nouveau-style brasseries in Paris. It shows that the model can be reproduced in New York with great flair.

6 medium ripe tomatoes, peeled

Pinch herbes de Provence

Fleur de sel and freshly ground
black pepper

5½ tablespoons extra virgin
olive oil

1 teaspoon good-quality balsamic
vinegar

8 ounces fairly dry-textured fresh
goat cheese

1 sheet frozen puff pastry,
preferably a brand made with
butter, thawed

2 bunches mâche greens

1 tablespoon red wine vinegar

2 tablespoons minced chives

Until recently, the only way to
peel tomatoes was to dip them
in boiling water for 30 seconds.
Now there is a new, inexpensive
paring tool with a serrated blade
that effectively and easily peels
tomatoes.

The liquid that drains from
the tomatoes may look watery,
but it's actually packed with flavor.
Save it to use in soups and sauces.
It can be frozen.

Cut each tomato in half lengthwise and, using your fingers, scoop out the seeds. Slice each half in thirds lengthwise. Place the tomatoes in a bowl and gently toss them with herbes de Provence, salt and pepper to taste, and 3 tablespoons of the olive oil. Allow them to marinate for at least 2 hours at room temperature. Before assembling the tarte, drain the tomatoes in a colander over a bowl to remove excess fluid.

Preheat the oven to 350 degrees. Brush a 9-inch pie pan, preferably glass, with ½ tablespoon of the oil. Arrange the tomato slices in it. Drizzle with the balsamic vinegar and top with crumbled goat cheese. Cut the puff pastry to fit the pan, allowing about an inch of overhang. Cover the tomatoes with the pastry, tucking the edges into the pan.

Bake the tarte for about 30 minutes, or until the crust is golden brown. Meanwhile, place the mâche in a bowl and toss it with the remaining olive oil and the wine vinegar. Add the chives, toss again, and set aside.

When the tarte is done, let it cool on a rack for 15 minutes. Place a serving plate over the pan and turn the tarte out onto the plate. Serve immediately with salad.

A white from Alsace, especially one with a touch
of fruity sweetness, like a gewürztraminer

SEARED FOIE GRAS WITH ASIAN PEAR– ENDIVE SALAD

THE GROCERY

The Grocery, a modest storefront that has had a happy following on Brooklyn's Smith Street in Carroll Gardens since 1999, captured the attention of the entire New York dining world. Its food received a top rating in one edition of the Zagat Survey, right up there with such esteemed venues as Le Bernardin and Daniel. The owners, Charles Kiely and Sharon Pachter, were stunned and thrilled. Despite a rush of reservations, the couple, who met when they were cooking at Savoy in Manhattan (page 203) and whose food expresses the same market-fresh point of view they shared at Savoy, are staying the course. They are maintaining the understated yet warm and welcoming atmosphere that made The Grocery so praiseworthy in the first place.

SERVES 4

2 tablespoons coarsely chopped skinned hazelnuts

4 slices brioche bread

1 Asian pear

1 endive

2 tablespoons sherry vinegar

¼ cup hazelnut oil

Sea salt and freshly ground black pepper

1 pound raw duck foie gras

2 tablespoons quince, apple cider, or apple jelly

¼ cup duck or chicken stock

1 teaspoon extra virgin olive oil

¼ cup oloroso sherry

½ tablespoon unsalted butter

Lightly toast the hazelnuts and set aside. Lightly toast the brioche and set aside.

Peel, quarter, and core the Asian pear. Cut each quarter into ⅛-inch-thick slices, stack them, and slice into ⅛-inch-thick matchsticks. Place in a large bowl. Quarter the endive lengthwise, slice out the core, then slice diagonally into ¼-inch-thick slivers. Place in the bowl with the Asian pear. In a small bowl whisk the vinegar and hazelnut oil together and season with salt and pepper.

Using a knife dipped in hot water, cut the foie gras into ½-inch-thick slices. You should get 8 slices. Use the tip of a sharp knife to pick out any bits of vein that show. Lightly score one side of each slice in a crosshatch pattern.

A few minutes before serving, have a warm platter ready beside the stove. Whisk the sherry vinegar dressing and toss with the Asian pear and endive slivers. Divide the salad among 4 generously sized warm salad plates, placing it off center. Place a slice of the brioche alongside the salad.

One way to make sure the foie gras is not overcooked is to touch it lightly. It should feel as though the inside is still soft.

The salad is delicious on its own or served with cheese.

A full-bodied New Zealand sauvignon blanc from Marlborough, or a dry sémillon

Place the jelly and the stock in a small saucepan and warm just until the jelly melts. Set aside. Heat a large, heavy skillet over high heat, brush with the olive oil, and when it just starts to smoke, place the foie gras slices in it, scored side down. Be careful not to crowd the pan; you may need to cook the foie gras in batches. Sear about 30 seconds, until browned, turn, and sear the other side about 30 seconds. Transfer to the warm platter. Do not overcook; it should be rare. Repeat, if necessary, to sear all the foie gras. Pour the sherry into the pan, whisk briefly, then pour in the jelly mixture. Cook over medium heat, stirring, a minute or so until syrupy. Whisk in the butter just until blended.

Use a spatula to transfer the slices of foie gras to the plates, placing them scored side up on the brioche, dust them lightly with sea salt, drizzle the sauce around, and scatter some of the hazelnuts on the plates. Serve at once.

SOUPS

WARM LENTIL SOUP WITH CRISP PANCETTA 50

CHICKEN SOUP 52

ONION SOUP GRATINÉE 53

VEGETABLE BREAD SOUP 54

SUNCHOKE SOUP WITH BLACK TRUMPET MUSHROOMS 56

OYSTER STEW 59

CHILLED SPRING PEA SOUP WITH PEA SALAD
AND MINTED CRÈME FRAÎCHE 60

WARM LENTIL SOUP WITH CRISP PANCETTA

Stacked, not sprawling, defines urban living, and Town, as its citified name suggests, complies with that concept. The restaurant, designed by David Rockwell, starts with a narrow bar at street level, then descends a couple of steps to an area with small tables for lounge dining, then on to the restaurant proper, resulting in a soaring atrium effect. Chef Geoffrey Zakarian's food is suitably urban-contemporary, calling on some inventive ingredients such as buckwheat and, in this creamy lentil puree, a moderately sweet, little-known French wine called *vin jaune.*

2½ cups (17.5 ounces) French
    Le Puy lentils

1 thick slice smoked bacon, diced

1 medium onion, peeled and
    chopped

1 carrot, peeled, in chunks

2 celery stalks, in chunks

2 thyme sprigs

1 bay leaf

1 head of garlic, halved horizontally

8 cups well-flavored chicken stock

2 tablespoons heavy cream

¼ cup *vin jaune* or medium-dry
    sherry (see tip, page 30)

1 tablespoon white wine vinegar

Salt and freshly ground black pepper

3 (¼-inch-thick) slices pancetta,
    cut into julienne

2 bunches scallions, trimmed and
    thinly sliced

French Le Puy lentils are
green instead of brown and
are smaller and somewhat nuttier-
tasting than American lentils.
They're what most chefs prefer.
Chefs also like to place a warm
garnish in the center of a bowl,
serve it , and then ladle the hot
soup over the garnish at the table.
It's a lovely way to serve a soup
that's worth remembering.

Place the lentils in a bowl, cover with cold water to a depth of 2 inches, and allow them to soak overnight. Drain.

In a large, heavy saucepan, gently sauté the bacon, and when it renders some of its fat, add the onion, carrot, celery, thyme, bay leaf, and garlic. Cook over medium-low heat until the vegetables are very tender, about 10 minutes. Drain the lentils, add them to the pot, cook a few minutes longer, then add the stock. Bring to a simmer, and cook gently until the lentils are very tender, about 40 minutes.

Remove a few tablespoons of the lentils and set aside. Remove garlic, thyme, and bay leaf. Transfer the contents of the pan to a food processor or blender and puree until smooth. You may have to do this in two batches. Pass the puree through a fine strainer. Clean the saucepan and add the puree to the pan. Bring the soup to a simmer, and add the cream, *vin jaune,* vinegar, and salt and pepper to taste. Remove from heat.

Heat a sauté pan, add the pancetta, and sauté until crisp. Add the scallions, allow them to wilt, then fold in the reserved lentils. Divide this mixture among 8 soup plates. Reheat the soup, thinning it with a little water if necessary, and ladle it over the pancetta mixture, then serve.

The wine in the soup, *vin jaune,* is a good accompaniment. In its place, an oloroso sherry will do nicely.

CHICKEN SOUP

> *These days "deli" often means a corner grocery.* But in New York restaurantese, a delicatessen is also a place to find a mile-high corned beef sandwich on rye with a sour pickle, smoky pastrami with a lush rim of fat, lox and eggs, and chicken soup. New Yorkers who have moved to far-flung places long for old-fashioned deli food, the contribution made by immigrant Jews from Eastern Europe more than 100 years ago. The Second Avenue Deli is one of the few remaining authentic sources, even though it lost its lease on Second Avenue in the East Village and moved to Murray Hill. It is still owned by the Lebewohl family. You can find foie gras almost anywhere now, but good chopped liver?

SERVES 8

1 pound chicken wings and drumsticks

2 celery stalks, cut into 3-inch pieces, including leaves

1 (3½- to 4-pound) chicken, rinsed

Kosher salt

1 large unpeeled onion, roots trimmed, and rinsed

1 large carrot, peeled

1 parsnip, peeled

Freshly ground white pepper

4 fresh dill sprigs, tied with string

The onion is left unpeeled because the skin adds a golden color to the soup.

For the clearest possible soup, line your strainer with a clean linen napkin.

Pour 3 quarts of cold water into a large stockpot. Add the chicken wings, drumsticks, and celery. Bring to a boil.

Rub the whole chicken inside and out with salt. Add it to the pot and boil for 5 minutes, skimming any residue that rises to the surface. Lower the heat to a simmer, cover, and cook until the whole chicken is cooked through, about 40 minutes. Transfer the whole chicken to a platter.

Add the onion, carrot, and parsnip to the pot, season with salt and pepper to taste, and simmer 1 hour and 15 minutes. Remove the carrot and set aside. Strain the contents of the pot into a clean saucepan, discarding the solids.

The whole chicken may be added to soup or reserved for chicken salad. If serving it in the soup, cut it up, and remove the skin and bones.

Dice the carrot and add it to the soup along with dill. Reheat, adding salt and pepper if needed. Remove the dill, ladle the soup into plates, and serve.

Wine? Beer? Not at all. The libation of choice in an old-fashioned deli is celery tonic.

ONION SOUP GRATINÉE

CAPSOUTO FRÈRES

For more than 20 years, Jacques Capsouto has welcomed those who seek French comfort food and are willing to venture south of Canal Street to his romantic restaurant in the semi-wilderness of the streets near the Holland Tunnel. Capsouto Frères has become inextricably woven into the fabric of New York, and despite its hip downtown location, it caters to those with a taste for more traditional fare. The Capsoutos' family tree is Sephardic-Jewish, and the Passover seders held annually in the restaurant are Illed to capacity. And when it comes to French comfort food, what could be better than a steaming bowl of rich onion soup paved with melted cheese on toast?

SERVES 6 TO 8

2 tablespoons unsalted butter
2 tablespoons vegetable oil
5 large onions, peeled and sliced thin
¼ cup brandy
¼ cup dry white wine
8 cups well-flavored beef stock
Salt and freshly ground black pepper
1 or 2 slices of toasted country bread
    or baguette for each serving
6 to 8 large slices Gruyère cheese

Instead of ladling the soup into individual bowls or crocks, it can be put into an ovenproof tureen or serving bowl, topped with all of the bread and cheese, then broiled until the cheese melts. Bring the tureen to the table and serve. But have a knife or even kitchen shears ready to cut through the stringy melted cheese as you serve each portion.

The soup is child's play. Begin by heating the butter and oil in a heavy 4- to 5-quart saucepan. Add the onions, and allow them to cook over medium-low heat, stirring from time to time, until they are meltingly soft and barely colored, 20 to 30 minutes. Do not rush this part of the preparation. Onions take time.

Add the brandy and wine, and cook them down until they have nearly evaporated. Add the stock and simmer for 30 minutes. Season with salt and pepper. The soup is ready to serve at this point, needing only its cap of bread and cheese, but there's no harm in setting it aside for several hours, or even refrigerating it overnight.

Reheat the soup if necessary and transfer it to individual ovenproof bowls or crocks. Top each with one or two slices of toast and cover the toast with the cheese. Preheat the broiler and run the bowls or crocks under it just until the cheese melts and bubbles. Serve at once.

 A Beaujolais cru, a Fleurie for example

VEGETABLE BREAD SOUP

Bill Telepan is one of those chefs who, in recent years, has put to rest the notion that great food and the Upper West Side are incompatible. He lives in the neighborhood himself. At his unpretentious but solidly grounded restaurant, his passion for local, seasonal ingredients is on full display and delights Lincoln Center concert-goers as well as his neighbors. His menu is studded with dishes, which, like this bread soup, rely on vegetables grown in the region. His wine list is also varied and richly endowed with unusual, reasonably priced selections.

4 slices sourdough bread or ciabatta cut ¼ inch thick

½ cup extra virgin olive oil

4 tablespoons freshly grated Parmigiano Reggiano, plus more for serving

1 large bunch fresh basil, leaves removed, stems tied together, optional

½ onion, chopped

2 garlic cloves, minced

1 large carrot, peeled, in ¼-inch dice

1 small celery root, peeled, in ¼-inch dice

1 large white turnip, peeled, in ¼-inch dice

1 leek, well trimmed, in ¼-inch-thick slices

2 ½ quarts vegetable stock

1 piece of rind (about 1 by 4 inches) from a chunk of Parmigiano Reggiano

1 medium Yukon gold potato, peeled, in ¼-inch dice

1 cup freshly cooked or canned cranberry, borlotti, or cannellini beans

1 bunch green Swiss chard, heavy stems removed, leaves coarsely chopped

Salt and freshly ground pepper

1 cup pesto, prepared or homemade

A verdicchio from Italy or a rueda from Spain

Preheat the oven to 450 degrees. Drizzle the bread with ¼ cup of the olive oil and dust with the cheese. Place on a baking sheet and bake until golden brown, about 6 minutes. Remove from the oven, let cool and trim off the crusts. Cut each slice into ½-inch squares. Reserve. If using fresh basil, remove the leaves and tie the stems in a bundle using kitchen twine. Reserve the leaves for making the pesto, or for another use. Set the bundle of stems aside.

In an 8-quart pot, heat the remaining olive oil over medium-low heat. Add the onion and garlic and cook, stirring, until soft but not colored, about 5 minutes. Add the carrot, celery root, and turnip and cook for 5 minutes, until they start to soften. Add the leek and cook for 3 minutes more.

Add the basil stems, stock, and cheese rind. Bring to a simmer and cook for 20 minutes.

Add the potato and simmer for 10 minutes. Add the diced bread, the beans, and Swiss chard and simmer for another 5 minutes. Remove from the heat, discard the basil stems and Parmesan rind. Season with salt and pepper. At this point, if needed, the soup can be set aside for an hour or two and reheated just before serving.

Serve with pesto and Parmigiano Reggiano on the side.

If fresh basil is not available, another herb, like fresh oregano, marjoram, or even flat-leaf parsley, can be substituted. With these, stems and leaves can be used.

Do not discard the rind from the Parmigiano Reggiano as you use the cheese; save it in the refrigerator. Italians use it to season soups and stews.

For an extra-delicious way to serve this soup, enough to make it a main course for a brunch or supper, float a poached, farm-fresh egg on each portion.

SUNCHOKE SOUP WITH BLACK
TRUMPET MUSHROOMS

AQUAVIT

This Scandinavian restaurant on the ground floor of a midtown office building is almost a museum of classic Danish and Swedish modern design, especially the main dining room. In addition, there is a Swedish café near the entrance. Heading the kitchen is Marcus Samuelsson, a Swede who was originally from Ethiopia and who is bringing a global outlook to traditional dishes and ingredients such as herring platters and lingonberries—staples of the Scandinavian kitchen. Here you'll find herring sushi and Kobe beef paired with aquavit spirits infused with uncommon flavors.

3½ tablespoons unsalted butter

1 pound fresh sunchokes (Jerusalem artichokes), peeled and chopped

2 shallots, finely chopped

2 garlic cloves

½ pound Yukon gold potatoes, peeled and cut into ½-inch cubes

4 cups chicken stock

2 cups mild fish stock

½ cup dry white wine

2 bay leaves

4 Chinese dried black mushrooms

2 thyme sprigs

2 tablespoons crème fraîche

Salt and freshly ground white pepper

2 cups (about 8 ounces) fresh black trumpet mushrooms or fresh chanterelle mushrooms

2 tablespoons minced chives

½ teaspoon black truffle oil, optional

The dried Chinese black mushrooms add a great deal of flavor but are too woody to be pureed. The black trumpet mushrooms, a variety of chanterelle also called *Trompettes de la Mort* (trumpets of death, because of their color), are the chef's choice because of the stunning color contrast they provide. But other mushrooms, including regular chanterelles, can be used instead.

Melt 1 tablespoon of the butter in a large saucepan over medium heat. Add the sunchokes and sauté until they begin to soften, about 5 minutes. Add the shallots and garlic, sauté 2 minutes more, then add the potatoes. Add the chicken stock, fish stock, wine, bay leaves, dried mushrooms, and thyme. Bring to a boil, reduce heat, and simmer gently until the vegetables are very tender, about 25 minutes.

Remove the soup from the heat, and discard the bay leaves, thyme, and dried mushrooms. Add the crème fraîche and 2 tablespoons of the butter, and puree the soup in a food processor, blender, or in the pot using a hand-held blender. You may have to puree the soup in two batches if using a food processor or regular blender. Return the soup to the saucepan and reheat. Season with salt and pepper.

In a sauté pan heat the remaining ½ tablespoon of butter. Add the trumpet mushrooms, and sauté over high heat until they just start to wilt, about 1 minute. Add the chives, stir, and remove from heat. Divide the mushroom mixture among 6 shallow soup plates. Ladle the hot soup over and, if desired, garnish with a few drops of truffle oil. Serve at once.

 A white Châteauneuf-du-Pape

OYSTER STEW

Thanks to loving restoration work and sensitive realignment of its commercial space, Grand Central Terminal, the world's largest railway station, has recently become an important New York dining venue. But the Oyster Bar, located off the ramp that connects the upper and lower levels of the station, was there before the other fine restaurants now found in Grand Central. Its landmark interior, arched with Guastavino tilework, was where travelers who were about to step aboard the 20th Century Limited dined. And the restaurant remains most famous for its oysters on the half shell, its oyster stews, and its oyster panroasts, which are prepared in specially designed silver bowls that swivel to allow the cook to pour out the contents.

SERVES 2

2 thin slices white sandwich bread, crusts removed

½ cup clam broth or clam juice

2 tablespoons unsalted butter

1 teaspoon Worcestershire sauce

½ teaspoon celery salt

12 oysters, shucked, with their liquor

1½ cups half-and-half

1 teaspoon sweet Hungarian paprika

Add 2 tablespoons of Heinz chile sauce just after the oysters have been added, replace the half-and-half with ½ cup heavy cream, and you'll have an oyster panroast instead of oyster stew.

Toast the bread. You'll want it on the dark side so it will add a bit of smoky flavor to the stew. Place each slice of the toast in a shallow soup plate. Now it's minutes until the dish is ready to serve.

Combine the clam broth, butter, Worcestershire sauce, and celery salt in the top of a double boiler set over boiling water. When the mixture is hot and the butter has melted, add the oysters and their liquor, and allow to cook for 30 seconds. Add the half-and-half, and cook just until the mixture is hot, then use a slotted spoon to transfer the oysters to the plates, placing 6 on each slice of toast. Ladle the cream mixture over the oysters, sprinkle with the paprika, and serve without delay.

 A pinot noir from Oregon or from Sonoma

CHILLED SPRING PEA SOUP WITH PEA SALAD AND MINTED CRÈME FRAÎCHE

OLIVES

> *Todd English first came on the scene* with a tiny restaurant in Charlestown, Massachusetts, on the edge of Boston. He has since turned Olives, as the restaurant is called, into an industry, with branches in Las Vegas, Washington, and New York. The settings vary but English's boldly flavored Mediterranean-style cooking is the hallmark of them all. The New York edition is in a stately former insurance company building-turned-hotel in the W chain.

SERVES 4

4 tablespoons extra virgin olive oil

1 medium onion, peeled and chopped

½ cup chopped celery

3 cups chicken stock or water

3 pounds fresh peas in the pod, shucked, about 3 cups shucked peas

½ cup sugar snap peas, trimmed

½ cup snow peas, trimmed

4 tablespoons crème fraîche

1½ tablespoons chopped fresh mint

Juice of ½ lemon

Sea salt and freshly ground black pepper

Heat 3 tablespoons of the oil in a heavy saucepan. Add the onion and celery and cook over low heat until translucent. Add the stock and simmer about 5 minutes, then remove from the heat. Transfer to a bowl sitting in an ice-water bath to cool.

Bring a pot with 2 quarts of salted water to a boil, add the shucked peas and blanch for 3 minutes, until tender but still bright green. Use a slotted spoon to remove the peas and place them in the chilling bowl of stock. Add the sugar snaps and snow peas to the boiling water, blanch 2 minutes, then drain and allow to cool in a separate small bowl.

Remove ½ cup of the peas from the stock and add them to the mixture of sugar snaps and snow peas. Coat with the remaining tablespoon of olive oil. Set aside.

Place the stock mixture in a blender and puree. Add 1 tablespoon of the crème fraîche and ½ tablespoon of the mint, blend briefly, then transfer to a container and chill at least 1 hour.

Mix the remaining crème fraîche with the remaining mint and the lemon juice, and set aside.

To serve, check the seasonings of the pea soup, adding salt and pepper as needed. Place a mound of the whole pea mixture in the center of each of 4 soup plates, spoon the soup around it, and top with a dollop of the crème fraîche mixture.

A dry white Italian wine, preferably a vermentino or pinot grigio

SALADS

CLASSIC CAESAR SALAD 64

TOMATO SALAD WITH SHAVED FENNEL AND GORGONZOLA 66

DEVILED EGGS AND FRISÉE WITH WARM BACON VINAIGRETTE 68

GIGI SALAD 71

BEET SALAD WITH BEET VINAIGRETTE 72

GOI TOM, GRILLED SHRIMP SALAD 74

CLASSIC CAESAR SALAD

TAVERN ON THE GREEN

On the edge of Central Park, the historic Tavern on the Green combines the beautiful architectural details of the pavilions that dot the 150-year-old park with the exuberance of the late Warner LeRoy, who will always be remembered as the city's Barnum of dining, the most spectacular restaurant showman ever. His restoration of Tavern on the Green gave its interior a Victorian grandeur and populated its gardens with a topiary menagerie that glitters with lights. The food is designed to please young and old, visitors and residents, who flock to the restaurant for special occasions and weekend brunches.

3 egg yolks or ½ cup commercial
  mayonnaise

2 tablespoons Dijon mustard

4 garlic cloves, minced

6 anchovies, or more to taste,
  drained and mashed

⅓ cup lemon juice

Freshly ground black pepper

¾ cup extra virgin olive oil

1¼ cups freshly grated Parmigiano-
  Reggiano

2 heads romaine lettuce, trimmed,
  rinsed, dried, and torn into
  pieces

A Sancerre, especially the
Henri Bourgeois 2001

At Tavern on the Green, the salad
is made with romaine hearts that
are split but have part of the stem
left intact to hold them together.
The dressing is then spooned
around. That's fine when a single
portion is involved, but to assemble
several servings at home, it's easier
to use torn lettuce. It's up to you.

This dressing calls for raw egg yolks. If you feel that using them poses a risk—although you might consider that organic, free-range eggs are less likely to cause problems—you can omit them and substitute ½ cup of commercial mayonnaise, in which case reduce the oil to ½ cup.

Place the egg yolks, mustard, garlic, anchovies, and lemon juice in a food processor and whirl until smooth. Season with pepper. With the machine running, slowly pour in the oil through the feed tube to make a thick, creamy dressing. Add ¼ cup of the cheese and blend briefly. Set aside in the refrigerator.

Next make the Parmesan crisps, which take the place of traditional croutons. You'll need a baking sheet with a nonstick Silpat liner or a small but reliable nonstick skillet. If you have a liner, place it on a baking sheet and cover it with the remaining cup of grated cheese in a thin layer. Preheat the oven to 350 degrees, and bake the cheese until it has melted and turned golden brown. Remove the baking sheet from the oven, allow it to cool, then break up the cheese into 1-inch pieces and set aside. An alternate method is to place a small nonstick skillet over medium heat, spread about ½ cup of the cheese evenly over the bottom, and cook it until the cheese melts and starts to brown. Remove the skillet from the heat, allow it to cool, and use a spatula to lift off and break up the layer of crisp cheese. Repeat the process with the remaining cheese.

To assemble the salad, put the lettuce in a big bowl. Give the dressing a quick whisk and pour it over the greens and toss. Consider using your hands, which are the most effective utensils of all. Scatter the cheese crisps over the top and serve.

TOMATO SALAD WITH SHAVED FENNEL AND GORGONZOLA

GOTHAM BAR & GRILL

Gotham Bar & Grill was meant to be a trendsetter when it opened. Housed in a handsome, soaring loft space on the edge of Greenwich Village, it was dedicated to cutting-edge American food. It almost did not make it. But then the owners hired Alfred Portale, a Culinary Institute of America graduate who had trained in France. They made a daring move introducing him and their restaurant to an uptown crowd by opening for a charity dinner for 200 people—who wound up loving the food and the restaurant. A loyal following soon developed. For his part, Portale capitalized on the *haute* in haute cuisine with towering presentations. He was devoted to the nearby Greenmarket, and his commitment to the farmers has influenced a generation of chefs, including Bill Telepan, the chef and owner of Telepan (page 54–55).

1 small fennel bulb

3 pounds assorted heirloom toma-
    toes of varying sizes and colors

Salt and freshly ground black pepper

½ cup finely chopped red onion

1 garlic clove, peeled and mashed
    to a paste with salt

2 teaspoons fresh thyme leaves

⅓ cup extra virgin olive oil

1 tablespoon aged red wine vinegar

1 tablespoon balsamic vinegar, aged
    at least 10 years

½ pound *haricots verts*, trimmed

2 tablespoons minced chives

2 cups loosely packed baby arugula
    or regular arugula (leaves only),
    rinsed and dried

5 ounces crumbled Gorgonzola

To slice the fennel, use a light-
weight, inexpensive Japanese-
style mandoline or a heavy-duty
French one if you prefer.

Plan on serving this salad when
ripe tomatoes are in season and
sold at farmers' markets.

Ice water is the secret ingredient in this recipe, used to crisp
and curl the fennel and, as chefs
say, to "shock" the cooked beans so
they keep their color.

Cut the fennel into ⅛-inch-thick slices vertically, and place in a bowl of ice water. Refrigerate for 1 hour.

Cut the tomatoes into slices, wedges, or halves, depending on their size and shape; you want pieces that will fit on a fork and are not much larger than bite-size. Place the tomatoes in a bowl and season with salt and pepper. Scatter the onion, garlic, and thyme on top. Whisk together the oil and vinegars, and drizzle on the tomatoes. Set aside for 15 minutes.

Bring a small saucepan of salted water to a boil, add the *haricots verts*, and cook until bright green, about 4 minutes. Drain and plunge the *haricots verts* into a bowl of ice water to stop the cooking. Drain and set aside.

Add the chives to the tomatoes and toss gently. Place the arugula in the center of 6 salad plates. Using a slotted spoon, lift the tomatoes and onions out of the bowl, allowing the dressing to drain off, and place them on the arugula, mounding them as high as possible. Arrange the *haricots verts* around the tomatoes. Drain the fennel and arrange it around the *haricots verts*. Sprinkle the Gorgonzola on top, spoon the dressing left in the bowl on the *haricots verts* and fennel, and serve.

A rich sauvignon blanc from New Zealand, is an excellent complement, although a summery rosé that's not too sweet would work well, too.

DEVILED EGGS AND FRISÉE WITH WARM BACON VINAIGRETTE

RELISH

Hip new neighborhoods need hip new places to eat. Relish, in Williamsburg, Brooklyn, fits the bill. Diner-style with dim, lounge-like lighting, a lovely indoor patio, and food best described as trendy American, it seems to satisfy the skinny young jeans-and-black-clad patrons. A frisée salad with eggs is typical bistro fare, but here it has been crossed with comfort food, deviled eggs substituting for poached. It can be hors d'oeuvres—pick off the deviled eggs first—a starter or, for some, dinner.

6 hard-cooked eggs, peeled and halved

1 teaspoon coarse (whole-grain) mustard

3 tablespoons mayonnaise

¼ teaspoon paprika

Salt and freshly ground black pepper

4 slices bacon

6 tablespoons extra virgin olive oil

2 teaspoons Dijon mustard

2 tablespoons white wine vinegar

1 tablespoon minced red onion

2 tablespoons minced chives

2 teaspoons chopped fresh tarragon leaves

2 small heads frisée, cored, rinsed and dried

10 cherry tomatoes, cut in half

> Why not triple the recipe for the eggs and serve them—without the salad—with drinks?

Unlike the classic bistro salad, *frisée aux lardons,* Relish's version without poached eggs is very easy to prepare. To make the deviled eggs: scoop the yolks into a bowl, mash them with the coarse mustard, mayonnaise, paprika and a touch of salt and pepper. Pile this mixture back into the whites, put the eggs on a plate, cover, and set them aside in the refrigerator. (Try to resist eating a couple of them on the spot. You may, but then you won't get any later.)

Fry the bacon, drain it on paper towels, and chop it. To the fat in the pan add the oil, Dijon mustard, vinegar, onion, 1 tablespoon of the chives, and the tarragon. Return the chopped bacon to the pan.

Pile the frisée in a salad bowl and toss it with the rest of the chives and the tomatoes. This is far as you can go in advance. If you're not serving this right away, put the salad in the refrigerator.

Minutes before you're about to serve the salad, warm the dressing in the pan, stirring it, and season to taste with salt and pepper—you will not need much. Pour the warm dressing over the frisée, toss it, and divide the salad among 6 plates. Top each with 2 deviled egg halves and serve.

 Bloody Marys

GIGI SALAD

The first Palm opened in New York in 1926. It is still owned by descendants of the founders, John Ganzi and Pio Bozzi, Italian immigrants who turned a spaghetti joint into a magnet for celebrities. The restaurant's name is a bureaucratic misspelling of the owners' intentions. They wanted "Parma." It became Palm, and it stuck. The walls are covered with cartoons of regulars, the oldest ones drawn by King Features Syndicate artists in exchange for dinner. Although the Palm is best known for steaks, the Gigi Salad is the dish that is ordered more than any other. It was named for its creator, the late Louis "Gigi" Delmaestro, who was the general manager of the Palm in West Hollywood for twenty-seven years. There is now a Palm Too across the street from the original, as well as a Palm West in the theater district and another in the financial district. Others are scattered across the country and in Mexico.

SERVES 4 TO 6

¼ pound bacon

2 tablespoons red wine vinegar

½ cup extra virgin olive oil

1 garlic clove, crushed

3 basil leaves, torn into pieces

1 pound fresh green beans, ends trimmed

1 pound (about 2) ripe beefsteak tomatoes, cored and cut into ½-inch chunks

1 medium sweet onion such as Vidalia, cut into ½-inch dice

Salt and freshly ground black pepper

½ pound jumbo or large shrimp, cooked, peeled, and cut into ½-inch-thick pieces

 An Australian chardonnay

Fry the bacon until crisp, drain on paper towels, and crumble. Set aside the crumbled bacon and discard the fat. Whisk the vinegar, oil, garlic, and basil in a bowl. Set aside.

Bring a quart of water to a boil, add the beans, and cook for 4 minutes. Drain the beans and run them under cold water until they are cool. Drain well, shaking off excess water, and spread them on paper towels to dry. Cut the beans into 1½-inch lengths.

Combine the beans, tomatoes, and onion in a salad bowl. Briefly whisk the vinaigrette, pour ½ cup of it over the vegetables, and toss. Add additional vinaigrette if needed, and season with salt and pepper.

Mound the salad on plates and top each serving with some of the shrimp and crumbled bacon. Serve at once.

> To make the West Coast variation of the salad, in addition top each serving with a hard-boiled egg, cut in quarters, and ½ of a peeled and diced Hass avocado.

BEET SALAD WITH BEET VINAIGRETTE

People love going to salad bars and picking and choosing, so why not give them the chance to design a whole meal that way? That was chef Tom Colicchio's concept: offer each component à la carte, making it possible to order, say, a main course of chicken or sea bass with a choice of several kinds of potatoes, grains, vegetables, and sauces. Customers resisted so the plates have become more fully composed, and for the really indecisive there is a prix fixe tasting menu. Even the design of the room emphasizes the craftsmanship of the materials—stone, wood, leather, and metal—and the tables are extra large, with plenty of room for the various copper pots and serving dishes that accumulate. The success of Craft has led to spin-offs: Craftbar, an Italian-style wine bar and restaurant, and 'Wichcraft, a chain of sandwich cafés. Craftsteak, in New York and other cities, has also been added.

SERVES 4

16 baby beets, each about 2 inches in diameter
2 tablespoons grapeseed oil
Kosher salt and freshly ground black pepper
1 cup extra virgin olive oil
1 large shallot, peeled and sliced
¼ cup red wine vinegar
½ teaspoon Dijon mustard

Preheat the oven to 325 degrees. Trim the roots and green tops from the beets. Scrub them to remove any soil.

Place the beets in a bowl, add the grapeseed oil, and toss the beets to coat. Season with salt and pepper. Wrap the beets in a sheet of heavy-duty foil. If using a variety of beets, wrap each color in a separate sheet of foil so they don't bleed onto each other. Place the foil pouches in a large roasting pan. Roast until tender, about 1 hour—a paring knife should penetrate easily. Remove the beets from the oven and let cool.

When the beets are cool enough to handle, rub off the outer skin with a paper towel. Set aside all but 3 beets. Coarsely chop the 3 beets and set them aside separately.

Heat 1 tablespoon of the olive oil in a skillet. Add the shallot, and cook over low heat until it's soft and translucent but not colored—the technique chefs call "sweating."

 Try to find an assortment of beets —golden, Chioggia (candy cane), and purple—to use in this recipe.

 Consider using disposable plastic gloves or even baggies when handling beets so you do not stain your hands.

Place the shallot in a blender jar with the vinegar, mustard, the chopped beets, and salt and pepper to taste. Puree the mixture, then add the remaining olive oil in a thin, steady stream.

Cut the reserved beets in half and arrange them on 4 plates. Drizzle with the beet vinaigrette and serve.

A rosé wine, preferably Greek, such as Xynómavro rosé

GOI TOM, GRILLED SHRIMP SALAD

LE COLONIAL

Le Colonial is the Catherine Deneuve of Vietnamese restaurants, presenting a lushly beautiful and decidedly romantic setting with lots of greenery, bamboo, and carved Asian woodwork. The second-floor lounge is even more lush. The menu gives a complete overview of the cooking of Vietnam, and the kitchen interprets that fresh yet complex cuisine with care. The crunch of lettuce, bean sprouts, and herbs contrasts with tender meats or fish charred on the grill. The flavors are at once herbaceous, fiery, and tart— an appetite-whetting combination if there ever was one.

SERVES 4

8 jumbo shrimp, shelled and
  deveined

1 teaspoon minced shallot

1 teaspoon minced garlic

2 tablespoons peanut oil

1 tablespoon Chinese oyster sauce

½ seedless English cucumber,
  peeled, halved lengthwise,
  and sliced paper thin

1 carrot, peeled and sliced paper thin

1 cup thinly sliced peeled daikon
  (long, white radish)

¼ cup thinly sliced red onion,
  separated into rings

1 teaspoon kosher salt

2 teaspoons *nuoc mam* (Vietnamese
  fish sauce), available in Asian
  stores

1 tablespoon sugar

1 tablespoon lime juice

2 teaspoons minced, seeded fresh
  red chile pepper

2 tablespoons extra virgin olive oil

2 tablespoons roughly chopped
  fresh basil leaves, preferably
  purple opal basil

1 tablespoon roughly chopped fresh
  mint leaves

2 tablespoons roasted unsalted
  peanuts, chopped

1 tablespoon fried shallots,
  optional (see tip)

Place the shrimp in a bowl and toss with the minced shallot, garlic, the peanut oil, and the oyster sauce. Set aside in the refrigerator to marinate for at least an hour.

Meanwhile, mix the cucumber, carrot, daikon, and onion in a bowl. In a separate bowl mix the salt, fish sauce, sugar, and lime juice together until the sugar dissolves. Add the chile pepper and whisk in the olive oil. Pour this dressing over the cucumber salad mixture and toss. Set aside.

Heat a grill or a griddle. Toss the shrimp with 1 tablespoon of the basil. Grill, turning once, until well-seared and cooked through. Mound the salad on a serving dish. Arrange the shrimp over it. Scatter the remaining basil, the mint, peanuts, and fried shallots on top and serve.

 Napa Valley chardonnay

Try to find the fried shallots. They are sold jarred in Asian shops and also online, from web sites that specialize in ethnic ingredients. They are also excellent to keep on hand to use as a crunchy garnish for other salads, baked potatoes, and eggs.

Le Colonial

PASTA & RISOTTO

SPAGHETTI CON POMODORINI 78

RIGATONI ALLA BUTTERA 80

LINGUINE WITH SALSA MONACHINA 82

PENNE GRATIN 83

SPAGHETTI WITH MUSSELS 84

RICOTTA AND SPINACH DUMPLINGS
WITH BUTTER AND SAGE 86

VERMICELLI GENGHIS KHAN 89

SMOKED TOMATO RISOTTO 90

RISOTTO WITH RADICCHIO AND SHRIMP 93

ENGLISH PEA RISOTTO 94

SPAGHETTI CON POMODORINI

CONVIVIO

Convivio is proof that New Yorkers will flock to any neighborhood for good food. Although Tudor City is on the edge of Midtown, it is an out-of-the-way enclave, one that has never been known for its restaurants. But Michael White, whose reputation as a first-rate interpreter of Italian food has been building over the years, and his partners, especially a wine expert, Chris Cannon, have changed all that. Sheer curtains and romantic candlelight soften the tailored room. In this setting, White's inventive pastas are not to be missed.

SERVES 4

½ cup extra virgin olive oil

4 cloves garlic, sliced thin

2 cups grape tomatoes, halved

1 cup roughly torn fresh basil leaves

Salt and freshly ground black pepper

1 pound spaghetti

⅓ cup freshly grated Parmigiano Reggiano

In a large skillet, heat the olive oil over medium heat until just warm. Add the sliced garlic, reduce the heat to low, and stir until soft but not colored, 2 or 3 minutes. Stir in the tomatoes and cook for 2 or 3 minutes, crushing them with a fork. Sprinkle the basil in and season with salt and pepper. Pour the sauce into a large, warm bowl.

Bring a large pot of salted water to a boil. Cook the spaghetti until al dente, 7 to 8 minutes. Drain. Add to the sauce, mix gently until well coated, and serve with the grated cheese on the side.

If grape tomatoes are not available, quartered cherry tomatoes can be substituted.

Tearing basil instead of cutting it helps keep it from darkening around the edges.

This dish is as delicious served at room temperature in summer as it is hot at other times of the year. You might want to add an extra drizzle of olive oil just before serving.

 An Etna rosso from Sicily

RIGATONI ALLA BUTTERA

Pino Luongo's restaurant empire has, for now, shrunk to this roomy Upper East Side outpost, since Coco Pazzo, Le Madri, and Tuscan Square have all closed. Still, one must not rule out the possibility that he will again expand his holdings in the future. At Centolire the menu is comfortable, as demonstrated by this richly creamy, sausage-studded pasta dish. The ease with which it can be assembled is certainly enough to recommend it to a home cook. But Mr. Luongo is a dedicated home cook himself, and his recipes are often like that.

½ pound hot Italian sausage, casing removed

½ pound sweet Italian sausage, casing removed

1 tablespoon unsalted butter

½ cup fresh or frozen garden peas

1 cup canned tomato puree

⅓ cup heavy cream

2 tablespoons freshly grated Parmigiano Reggiano

Salt and freshly ground pepper

1 pound rigatoni

Fresh garden peas can be used instead of frozen. You will need to shell about 1/2 pound, then blanch them for 3 minutes in boiling water before adding them to the sauce.

Italian cooks usually save a little of the pasta water, either just before draining the pasta, or from beneath the colander, then add it as needed when they finish the dish. Its value as an ingredient is its ability to smooth out or stretch a pasta sauce.

Other pasta shapes, including penne and strozzapreti, can be used in place of rigatoni.

Place a large, heavy skillet over medium heat. Add all the sausage meat, breaking it up with the back of a wooden spoon, and cook it, stirring, until it loses its redness and is uniformly crumbly. Transfer the sausage to a bowl.

Wipe the pan clean and add the butter over medium heat. When it melts, return the sausage to the pan and add the peas and the tomato puree. Mix well and cook until the sauce thickens and the peas are tender, 3 to 4 minutes. Add the cream and cook for 2 or 3 minutes. Add 1 tablespoon of the cheese to thicken the sauce. Stir until creamy and smooth. Add salt and pepper to taste. Remove from the heat.

Bring 4 quarts of salted water to a boil in a large pot, add the rigatoni, and cook until it is al dente, about 10 minutes. Drain, reserving ½ cup of the pasta water.

Place the skillet with the sauce over low heat, add the pasta to the skillet and toss gently. Sprinkle on the remaining cheese. Stir the pasta into the sauce for a few minutes, adding a little of the cooking water if necessary, then serve.

 A Tuscan red wine, a chianti or super-Tuscan

LINGUINE WITH SALSA MONACHINA

MARIO'S

Arthur Avenue is the main thoroughfare of the Belmont section, the Bronx's Little Italy. Old-fashioned pasta shops, bakeries, cheese shops, fish markets, and groceries still thrive. Mario's has been in business there since 1919. The fifth generation of the Migliucci family runs the restaurant. The specialties of the house are what have become known as "Italian-American" food—the Neapolitan-style cooking of immigrant families—that remains beloved in America. But it is not just spaghetti and meatballs at Mario's. More sophisticated fare, such as potato gnocchi and osso buco, are also on the menu. The Salsa Monachina in this recipe is the same as the popular puttanesca. Joseph Migliucci, one of the owners, says they use *monachina* because it is a more polite term than *puttanesca*, which means streetwalker.

SERVES 4 TO 6

1 (28-ounce) can San Marzano tomatoes

¼ cup salt-packed capers

3 salt-packed anchovies

¼ cup extra virgin olive oil

3 large garlic cloves, sliced thin

8 oil-cured black olives, pitted and sliced

Salt and freshly ground black pepper

1 pound dried linguine

Place the tomatoes in a large bowl and crush them with your hands. Rinse the capers and anchovies and pat dry.

Heat the oil over low heat in a 4-quart saucepan. Add the garlic and sauté until lightly browned. Stir in the capers and olives. Add the anchovies and stir until they dissolve. Add the tomatoes and their juice. Cook, stirring occasionally, about 1½ hours, until the sauce has thickened, darkened, and intensified. Season to taste with salt and pepper. Remove from the heat.

Bring a large pot of salted water to a boil for the linguine. Cook the pasta until it is al dente, about 6 minutes. Drain. Reheat the sauce and add the pasta to the sauce. Stir the pasta in the sauce for a few minutes, then serve.

 A pinot grigio if you like white, or Vino Nobile di Montepulciano for a red

> Capers that are packed in salt instead of vinegar, and anchovies that are packed in salt instead of oil, are plumper and have better flavor.

PENNE GRATIN

Fresco by Scotto is a family affair. It opened in 1993 and immediately attracted the power elite from politics and the entertainment world. Four members of the Scotto family are involved in the day-to-day operations, and you are likely to see one or more of them on hand at any time. Marion Scotto, the matriarch of the family, had a political background in Brooklyn; Rosanna Scotto is a television news anchor; Elaina Scotto, a former publicist, was in fashion; and Anthony Scotto Jr. came from the food service industry. Their restaurant is bright and lively, decorated with murals that illustrate the bounty of Italy. This dish, nicknamed Penne from Heaven, is Fresco's interpretation of macaroni and cheese.

SERVES 6

Salt
1 pound penne pasta
3 tablespoons extra virgin olive oil
6 ounces prosciutto, diced
2 tablespoons unsalted butter
1 cup half-and-half
9 ounces freshly grated
  Parmigiano-Reggiano
  (about 3 cups)
Freshly ground black pepper

> The penne can be prepared in advance and baked at the last minute. But it is best to transfer the mixture from the sauté pan to a bowl and refrigerate it, because the pasta may soak up too much sauce while it waits. Before transferring it to the baking dish and running it under the broiler, you may need to moisten it with another ½ cup of half-and-half.

Bring 4 quarts of salted water to a boil in a large pot. Cook the pasta until al dente, about 8 minutes. Drain and keep warm.

Preheat the broiler.

While pasta is cooking, heat the oil in a large sauté pan. Add prosciutto and sauté over low heat, stirring, until it loses its color. Add the butter. When the butter has melted, add the half-and-half, about 2 cups of the cheese, and freshly ground pepper to taste. Bring to a simmer, add the penne, and toss to mix. Transfer to a shallow baking dish. Sprinkle with the remaining cup of cheese.

Place under the broiler and broil about 5 minutes, until the top is golden. Serve at once.

 Vernaccia de San Gimignano

SPAGHETTI WITH MUSSELS

Fiamma is one of a large group of restaurants that caters to a youngish crowd. But unlike the others in restaurateur Stephen Hanson's portfolio (Dos Caminos, Ruby Foo's, Blue Water Grill, Park Avalon, Ocean Grill, Isabella's, Atlantic Grill, and even Blue Fin), Fiamma has succeeded in aiming high, especially with the chef Fabio Trabocchi in the kitchen. It's one of several outstanding Italian restaurants. It's a comfortable, well-appointed multi-story venue with inventive food that remains true to its Italian roots.

2½ cups dry white wine

3¼ pounds mussels, preferably Prince Edward Island, scrubbed and debearded

2 tablespoons extra virgin olive oil

3 garlic cloves, minced

3 large ripe tomatoes, peeled and coarsely chopped

1 pound spaghettini

3 tablespoons flat-leaf parsley leaves, coarsely chopped

Pasta dishes made with seafood are generally not served with cheese.

Be sure to provide a bowl on the table for discarded mussel shells.

Place a 4- to 6-quart pot over high heat and add the wine and the mussels. Reduce the heat to very low, cover, and cook until the mussels open, about 6 minutes. Scoop the mussels into a bowl. Discard any that have not opened. Cover and keep warm.

Pour the mussel broth through a fine-mesh strainer into a bowl.

Heat the olive oil in the mussel pot. Add the garlic and cook until soft but not brown, about 3 minutes. Add the tomatoes and cook for 5 minutes, stirring, until they start to soften. Add the mussel broth. Shell half the mussels and add them to the pot. Place the rest of the mussels in a colander or strainer over simmering water to keep them warm.

Bring 4 to 5 quarts of well-salted water to a boil in a large pot and add the spaghettini. Cook until al dente, about 6 minutes. Drain. Add the pasta to the mussel and tomato mixture and toss. Add the parsley. Divide the mussels among individual bowls, topping each portion with some of the mussels in their shells. Serve at once.

 A bone-dry sauvignon blanc from Le Marche region

RICOTTA AND SPINACH DUMPLINGS WITH BUTTER AND SAGE

FELIDIA

A beautifully appointed two-story town house restaurant is where Lidia Bastianich established a Manhattan beachhead after developing a following for her cooking in Queens. Her cuisine combines the food of her native Istria, the easternmost region of Italy, with high-end northern Italian specialties and hearty home cooking. A well-stocked cellar emphasizes the wines of Friuli, including some from the family's own vineyards. Bastianich has become an important culinary figure, and is one of too few women chefs who have outstanding restaurants in New York, like this one, and the grand Del Posto in the meatpacking district.

SERVES 10

2½ pounds whole-milk ricotta cheese

Salt

4 eggs, beaten

1 pound stemmed spinach leaves, cooked, squeezed dry, and finely chopped

¾ cup freshly grated Parmigiano-Reggiano, plus extra for serving

6 tablespoons fine dry bread crumbs

3 to 4 cups all-purpose flour

Freshly ground black pepper

1½ cups chicken broth

5 tablespoons unsalted butter

10 fresh sage leaves

Place the ricotta in a sieve lined with cheesecloth set over a bowl. Cover with plastic wrap and allow to drain in the refrigerator for 8 to 24 hours. This removes the excess moisture from the ricotta so the dumplings will hold their shape.

Bring a large pot of salted water to a boil.

In a medium mixing bowl combine the eggs, drained ricotta, spinach, 6 tablespoons of the Parmigiano-Reggiano, bread crumbs, and 4 tablespoons of the flour. Season with salt and pepper.

Dust a baking sheet generously with some of the flour. Line a second baking pan with a lightly-floured kitchen towel. With floured hands, roll about 2 tablespoons of the ricotta mixture into a ball about 1½ inches in diameter. Roll it in the baking sheet of flour until well-coated. Test by dropping it into boiling water. It should hold its shape and rise to the surface within a minute. Cook another minute, then remove with a slotted spoon. If the dumpling does not hold its shape, add some more flour to the mixture and test again. Taste, and adjust seasonings if necessary.

The pound of spinach amounts to about 20 cups, loosely packed. Be sure it is well rinsed to remove all sand and grit.

The dumplings are called gnudi, meaning naked, because they essentially consist of spinach-ricotta filling without any surrounding pasta.

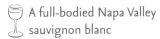

A full-bodied Napa Valley sauvignon blanc

Form remaining mixture into balls, roll in flour, and set on the lightly floured towel.

In a skillet large enough to hold all the dumplings in a single layer, heat the broth, butter, and sage leaves until just simmering. Simmer for 3 minutes, then remove from heat. If you do not have a skillet large enough, divide the sauce ingredients between two skillets or prepare the dish in two batches.

Place half the dumplings in the pot of boiling water and stir gently until they rise to the surface, about 1 minute. Cook until firm, about 1 minute more. Remove with a skimmer, drain, and transfer to the skillet with the sage sauce. Cook the remaining dumplings and add them to the skillet. Place the skillet over medium-low heat and gently shake the pan to coat the dumplings with sauce. Remove the pan from the heat, add the remaining 6 tablespoons of cheese, and swirl the dumplings in the sauce until they are coated. Serve in bowls, spooning any extra sauce over them. Pass additional cheese alongside.

VERMICELLI GENGHIS KHAN

It only takes one city block, but from the hustle and bustle of Little Korea (West 32nd Street from Fifth to Sixth Avenues), one can step out of one's shoes—literally—and into the peaceful serenity of Hangawi. It is a vegetarian Korean restaurant, with a Buddhist philosophy and food that explores the seemingly infinite possible uses for burdock, sweet potato, tofu, and other nonmeat ingredients. Korean teas, including rare wild green teas, are another specialty. A spin-off called Franchia, which specializes in teas and light food, including noodle dishes, salads, and dumplings, is another welcoming oasis nearby.

SERVES 4

6 ounces *jap chae* (Korean dried sweet potato vermicelli)

¼ cup soy sauce

1 tablespoon sake

1 tablespoon Asian sesame oil

2 tablespoons dark brown sugar

1 tablespoon grated fresh ginger

3 ounces fresh shiitake mushrooms, stemmed and sliced thin

4 ounces oyster mushrooms, stems trimmed, torn in strips

4 ounces cremini mushrooms, sliced thin

1 small onion, sliced thin vertically

1 small zucchini, trimmed, quartered lengthwise, and cut in thirds

1 cup broccoli florets

12 snow peas, trimmed

2 cups sliced napa cabbage

1 carrot, peeled and slant-cut into ½-inch slices

2 scallions, trimmed and cut into 1-inch lengths

Place the noodles in a large bowl, cover with warm water, and allow to soak at least 2 hours. Drain well.

Combine the soy sauce, sake, sesame oil, brown sugar, and ginger in a wok or large sauté pan. Add 1 cup water. Bring to a simmer and cook over very low heat about 5 minutes, stirring. Stir in the drained noodles and the remaining ingredients. Cook, stirring over low heat, about 10 minutes, until the mushrooms have wilted and the other vegetables are tender but still bright-colored. Transfer to a platter and serve.

Nongju, a milky Korean rice wine traditionally served in a ceramic pot with a gourd as a ladle. Green tea or sake are also suitable.

Korean vermicelli is sold in Korean supermarkets and some other Asian stores. Chinese glass or cellophane noodles can be substituted.

SMOKED TOMATO RISOTTO

When Restaurant Associates opened the Brasserie in 1959 in the Mies van der Rohe–designed Seagram Building, it was a revelation. It served breakfast and dinner, and was open around the clock, providing a classy alternative to the neighborhood diner. It's had its ups and downs since then, and after having been closed for several years, was reinaugurated after a complete redesign. It is owned by Patina Restaurant Group, which also runs the restaurants in most of the city's museums and concert halls, as well as Sea Grill and Rock Center Café in Rockefeller Center. It's very modern now, designed by Diller + Scofidio and done mostly in pale, glowing, translucent greens. The food, too, has moved from a mostly French brasserie style to a more international menu. It still offers many brasserie favorites such as handsome seafood platters, steak-frites, and mussels; but there are Asian touches in some of the seasonings; and Italian, too, such as this risotto, with its cutting-edge smoked tomatoes to brighten the dish and play their subtle flavor off the piney touch of rosemary.

8 medium ripe plum tomatoes, halved lengthwise and seeded

5 tablespoons extra virgin olive oil

1 tablespoon balsamic vinegar

5 garlic cloves, minced (about 1½ teaspoons)

Salt and freshly ground black pepper

3 fresh rosemary sprigs

2 tablespoons unsalted butter

1 small yellow onion, peeled and minced

2 shallots, peeled and minced

1 cup Italian rice, preferably Carnaroli or Arborio

1 cup dry white wine

2 cups well-seasoned chicken stock

⅓ cup freshly grated Parmigiano-Reggiano

2 tablespoons fresh thyme leaves

The tomatoes are not literally smoked, but acquire their smokiness from the high heat in the pan. It's a good idea to turn on your kitchen exhaust or open a window while you smoke the tomatoes. If you have a small stove-top smoker, you can use it for the tomatoes. But do not overdo it; 5 minutes are enough.

Place the tomatoes in a bowl with 3 tablespoons of the oil, the vinegar, 1 teaspoon of the minced garlic, and salt and pepper to taste. Mix everything thoroughly and set it aside for an hour.

Heat a large cast-iron skillet until it starts to smoke. Put two sprigs of the rosemary in it, and when the herb is fragrant and starts to brown, add the marinated tomatoes, cut side down. Remove from the heat, cover the pan, and set it aside for about 20 minutes or so.

Heat the remaining 2 tablespoons of the oil and the butter in a heavy 3-quart saucepan. Add the rest of the garlic, the onion, and shallots, and sauté everything, stirring over medium heat, until the vegetables are soft. Stir in the rice and cook it about 1 minute, until it starts to whiten. Pour in ½ cup of the wine and cook, stirring, until the wine is absorbed by the rice. Repeat with the rest of the wine. Meanwhile, heat the chicken stock in a small saucepan. After the wine has been absorbed, start adding the chicken stock ½ cup at a time, stirring and adding more as it is absorbed.

By the time all the broth is used up, the rice should be al dente. Fold in the cheese and season to taste with salt and pepper. Add the smoked tomatoes along with any liquid in the skillet. Strip the leaves from the remaining sprig of rosemary and fold those in, too, along with the thyme leaves. At this point the rice should be creamy and ready to serve. You do not need additional grated cheese.

White St. Joseph from the Rhône or a viognier

RISOTTO WITH RADICCHIO AND SHRIMP
ANTONUCCI

Francesco Antonucci, from Venice, first attracted attention at Remi, a kind of Venetian fantasy in Midtown. But Remi was sold, so the chef moved to more modest premises on the Upper East Side. The food is no longer strictly Italian, much less Venetian, but guests are welcomed with a dish of warm goat cheese and tomato, just as they were at Remi. The restaurant, its walls hung with artworks by the chef's friends, is, in many respects, the ultimate neighborhood gathering spot, a solid fixture, but the food is so well prepared that the place attracts attention from around the city.

SERVES 4

Salt

20 large shrimp, shelled and deveined

6 tablespoons unsalted butter

1 medium onion, peeled and minced

1 cup Italian short-grain rice, preferably Vialone Nano or Arborio

5 cups (approximately) well-seasoned fish stock

½ cup dry white wine

10 to 12 leaves radicchio, preferably the long Treviso variety, chopped

1 tablespoon Cognac

Freshly ground black pepper

1 tablespoon finely chopped flat-leaf parsley leaves

> In the Venice area, Vialone Nano, which is slightly more slender than Arborio and makes the risotto a trifle moister, is preferred. A good Venetian risotto is called *alla onda,* or wavy.

Bring 2 quarts of well-salted water to a boil. Add the shrimp, cook 30 seconds, then drain them.

In a heavy 3-quart sauce pan, melt 4 tablespoons of the butter. Stir in the onion and sauté over low heat until it's translucent. Add the rice and allow it to cook about 1 minute, stirring, until it begins to whiten. Meanwhile, bring the fish stock to a simmer in a separate saucepan.

Add the wine to the rice, stir, and cook until it is nearly absorbed. Stir in the radicchio. Begin adding the fish stock, about ½ cup at a time, stirring fairly steadily, and adding additional stock as it becomes absorbed by the rice. Just keep the saucepan at a steady simmer and the rice will soak up the stock. After about 15 minutes, when all but about ½ cup of the stock is used, the rice will be nearly tender. Fold in all but 4 of the shrimp. Stir, and add the remaining stock. The rice should be al dente and creamy, in an almost-sauce. Fold in the Cognac and the remaining 2 tablespoons of butter and season to taste with salt and pepper.

Divide the risotto among 4 plates, top each with a reserved shrimp, and sprinkle with parsley. Serve hot.

 Chilled, sparkling prosecco

ENGLISH PEA RISOTTO

Although Petrossian is best known as the New York branch of the French caviar house, and dining in its opulent headquarters invariably means beginning with caviar or foie gras, the restaurant offers much more. Refined service and elegantly appointed tables provide the setting for finely wrought contemporary French food. Should caviar be the mealtime requirement, it will be served in a special *presentoir*, with silver and vermeil paddles for spooning it up. Petrossian's caviars range from the finest beluga to American farm-raised transmontanus, which today can stand up to sevruga.

SERVES 4

4 cups (approximately) vegetable stock

2 cups shucked garden peas, about 2 pounds peas in the pod

Salt and freshly ground black pepper

4 tablespoons (½ stick) soft unsalted butter

1 medium onion, finely minced

4 garlic cloves, finely minced

1 cup rice for risotto, preferably Vialone Nano or Arborio

2 cups fruity white wine such as riesling

2 teaspoons chopped rosemary leaves

½ cup freshly grated Parmigiano-Reggiano

> The risotto can be garnished with fresh pea shoots.

Heat ¾ cup of the vegetable stock in a small saucepan until just warmed. Place it in a blender jar, add 1 cup of the peas, and puree. Season to taste with salt and pepper and set aside.

Bring 2 cups of water to a boil in a small saucepan. Add remaining peas and cook for 2 minutes. Drain and chill in a bowl of ice water. Heat the remaining vegetable stock and keep at a simmer.

In a 3- to 4-quart saucepan, melt 1 tablespoon of the butter over medium heat. Add the onion and garlic and sauté until soft but not brown. Add the rice and stir until it begins to whiten. Add the wine and cook until it just moistens the rice mixture. Add half the vegetable stock. Cook, stirring, over low heat, until most of the stock has been absorbed. Add another cup of the remaining stock and cook, stirring, until it has been absorbed by the rice. By this time the rice should be nearly al dente. Continue to add the stock until the rice is al dente but not hard. Fold in the pea puree and the remaining butter and cook, stirring, until the mixture is creamy. Season to taste with salt and pepper. Fold in the cooked peas, rosemary, and cheese. Serve at once.

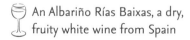 An Albariño Rías Baixas, a dry, fruity white wine from Spain

EGGS, SANDWICHES, PIZZA & BRUNCH

OEUFS COCOTTE

There are dozens of New York restaurants that call themselves brasseries—even one that has a lock, pure and simple, on the name Brasserie. But none captures the atmosphere of Paris's glorious Belle Époque and Art Deco dining halls like Keith McNally's Balthazar in SoHo. The name itself evokes Balzar, one of the most beloved of the Left Bank places. And truth be told, New York's Balthazar is lovelier by far than that particular Parisian model. It took an Englishman, not a Frenchman, to accomplish it. McNally brought some of the details for his tile, brass, and dark wood dining room—a former leather goods wholesale store—from France, but many of the fittings, like the mirrors showing their age, came from antiques markets in this country. McNally has a similar way with evocative decor at Pravda, his vodka-and-caviar bar. At Balthazar, from the raw bar selections to the steak with terrific frites to the warm apple tart, the food is exactly what one expects, enhanced by fresh bread from the restaurant's own bakery (there's a retail shop adjacent). And for those in the know, breakfast at Balthazar is a true treasure: relaxed, low-key, and delicious. And not just for indulgences like the croissants, but also for specialties like perfectly scrambled eggs and McNally's favorite Oeufs Cocotte, eggs baked in ramekins with cream and fresh thyme.

SERVES 4

1 tablespoon soft unsalted butter

4 tablespoons freshly grated Parmigiano-Reggiano

1 teaspoon fresh thyme leaves

Salt and freshly ground black pepper

½ cup heavy cream

8 eggs, organic if possible

4 fresh thyme sprigs

Toast or grilled bread, for serving

 Good coffee or a mimosa

Preheat the oven to 325 degrees. Butter 4 shallow 1-cup round or oval ovenproof ramekins. Sprinkle each with ½ tablespoon of the cheese and ¼ teaspoon of thyme leaves. Lightly dust with salt and pepper. Place ramekins in a baking pan at least 2 inches deep.

Spoon 2 tablespoons of the cream into each ramekin. Break 2 eggs into each ramekin and season with salt and pepper. Sprinkle on the remaining cheese and lay a thyme sprig on top. Pour hot water into the baking pan to come halfway up the sides of the ramekins. Carefully place the baking pan in the oven and bake 8 to 10 minutes, until the whites are just set and the cream and cheese are bubbling and lightly browned. Serve at once, with toast or grilled bread.

CALIFORNIA OMELET

Michael McCarty was among the first to bring California cuisine, with its salads, bright vegetables, and free-range chicken to Manhattan, opening a branch of his Santa Monica restaurant in Midtown. It's a comfortable, understated room enlivened with fine modern art, including paintings by McCarty's wife, Kim. A power crowd, mostly in publishing, are the regulars at breakfast, lunch, and dinner. The menu emphasizes fresh ingredients, organic when available.

SERVES 1 TO 2

3 strips thick-cut smoked bacon

1 tablespoon unsalted butter

2 tablespoons minced onion

3 button mushrooms, sliced

1 tablespoon clarified butter or extra virgin olive oil

3 eggs, beaten until frothy

Salt and freshly ground black pepper

¼ Hass avocado, sliced thin

1 sun-dried tomato, chopped

1 tablespoon sour cream

 Fresh blood orange juice

It is important to keep the eggs moving in the pan so they do not take on any color.

Fry the bacon until crisp. Drain well, chop, and set aside. Discard the fat from the pan.

In a 9-inch nonstick skillet, melt the butter. Add the onion and sauté over low heat until the onion is translucent. Add the mushrooms and sauté until they have softened and are barely beginning to brown, about 5 minutes. Remove from the heat. Transfer onions and mushrooms to a plate and set aside.

Wipe out the pan. Add the clarified butter or oil and place over medium heat. Season the eggs with salt and pepper and pour them into the pan. Working quickly with a heat-proof rubber spatula, move the outer edges to the center, allowing the uncooked egg to run to the outside. The cooked egg will pile up in the middle of the pan. When very little of the still-liquid egg remains in the pan, place the mushrooms and onion on half of the egg mixture, on the far side of the pan. Place the chopped bacon, avocado, tomato, and sour cream on top of the mushrooms and onion. Use your spatula to fold the plain half of the omelet over the filled half. Roll the omelet out of the pan onto a plate and serve at once.

PANZEROTTI

The majority of Italian restaurants in New York are what you might consider generalists—that is, they have menus of fairly commonplace dishes that enjoy abiding popularity. But, increasingly, places that keep faith with a particular region are opening. I Trulli, named for the odd stone structures that dot the landscape of Puglia in southeastern Italy, is one of these. Panzerotti are festive fried half-moon turnovers filled with fresh mozzarella, tomatoes, and anchovies, iconic ingredients from this sunny part of Italy. They are served with a glass of wine before dinner, to whet the appetite.

SERVES 16

1 package active dry yeast

Pinch of sugar

3½ tablespoons extra virgin olive oil

Sea salt and freshly ground black
  pepper

3 cups flour, approximately

½ pound ripe plum tomatoes,
  peeled and coarsely chopped

4 ounces fresh mozzarella, cut in
  16 pieces

2-ounce tin flat anchovies, drained
  and chopped

1½ to 2 cups vegetable oil,
  for deep-frying

In a large bowl dissolve the yeast and sugar in ¼ cup warm water. Set aside to proof for about 5 minutes. Add 3 tablespoons of the olive oil, ½ teaspoon salt, several grinds of fresh pepper, and 1 cup warm water. Add most of the flour, ½ cup at a time, stirring with a wooden spoon until a dough forms that leaves the sides of the bowl. Turn the dough out onto a lightly floured work surface and knead for about 8 minutes, until it is smooth and springy, adding flour as needed to keep it from being too sticky. Shape the dough into a ball.

Brush a bowl that is about twice the size of your ball of dough with the remaining ½ tablespoon olive oil. Place the dough in the bowl and turn it so it becomes coated with oil on all sides. Cover it loosely and set it aside to rise until doubled, about 1 hour at room temperature, longer in the refrigerator.

Coarsely chop the tomatoes. Place them in a colander set over a bowl and sprinkle with salt. Let drain for 30 minutes.

When the dough has risen, divide it into quarters, then cut each quarter into 4 pieces. Place a piece of dough on a lightly floured work surface and cover the remaining pieces with an overturned bowl. Roll out the piece of

dough to a 4-inch circle. Place 1 teaspoon tomato and a piece each of mozzarella and anchovy to one side of the circle. Fold the other half of the dough over the filling to make a half-moon. Press out the air and pinch the edges firmly together to seal. Use a fork to seal them tight. Repeat with the remaining ingredients.

In a deep, heavy saucepan or deep fryer, heat at least 1 inch of oil to 370 degrees on a frying thermometer, or until a 1-inch piece of bread dropped in the oil browns in 1 minute. Carefully slip the panzerotti, a few at a time, into the hot oil. Leave enough room between them so that they do not touch. Turn them once or twice and cook until golden brown, about 3 minutes.

Remove the finished panzerotti with tongs or a slotted spoon and place them on paper towels to drain. Serve hot.

 An aglianico del Vulture

TRE POMODORI PIZZA

SAPORI D'ISCHIA

Sapori D'Ischia started as an Italian import warehouse and wholesale distributor in Woodside, Queens. Then it opened its doors to the public for retail sales. Gradually it began adding a restaurant, first just pizza and some antipasto items at lunchtime. Eventually it became a full-fledged restaurant in the evening, with a menu of salads, oven-baked specialties, pastas, pizzas, main courses, and desserts. It is still rather out of the way, but the word is out and it has acquired a following of dedicated shoppers and diners.

½ package active dry yeast, approximately 1½ teaspoons

3 tablespoons extra virgin olive oil

2 teaspoons sea salt

1 cup cake flour

3 cups (approximately) bread flour

1 cup canned San Marzano tomatoes, drained

Freshly ground black pepper

2 cups cherry tomatoes, halved

10 Italian sun-dried tomatoes

1 cup (about 3 ounces) shaved Parmigiano-Reggiano

2 sprigs fresh basil

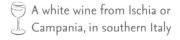 A white wine from Ischia or Campania, in southern Italy

Instead of simmering and seasoning the San Marzano tomatoes, Sapori D'Ischia recommends simply buying their own brand of tomato sauce made with San Marzano tomatoes, the best Italian canned tomatoes.

Place the yeast, 1½ tablespoons of the oil, and 1 teaspoon of the salt in a large mixing bowl. Stir in 1⅓ cups warm water. Use a wooden spoon to stir in the cake flour. Add the bread flour, ½ cup at a time, until a soft dough forms and begins to pull away from the sides of the bowl. You should have added a total of 3 to 3½ cups of flour at this point. Spread the last ½ cup of bread flour on a work surface and knead the dough, adding additional flour as necessary, until a soft, pliable dough has formed that's not sticky. Shape it into a ball, cover it with a towel, and allow to rest 10 minutes.

Divide the dough into 2 equal balls, brush them lightly with a little of the remaining olive oil, cover them with a clean towel, and set aside to rise for about 1 hour, until doubled.

While the dough is rising, crush the San Marzano tomatoes and place in a nonreactive saucepan. Bring to a simmer, add the remaining oil, and season with the remaining teaspoon of salt and pepper to taste. Remove from the heat.

Preheat the oven to 500 degrees. Set the oven rack to the lowest position. Punch down one ball of the dough and knead briefly. Stretch and roll it into a very thin, 10-inch round. Place it on a pizza stone or a pizza pan. Spread it with half of the tomato sauce and scatter half of the cherry tomatoes on top. Bake about 10 minutes or longer, if needed, until the crust is golden brown. Strew half of the sun-dried tomatoes, half of the Parmigiano-Reggiano, and half of the basil over the pizza and serve at once. Bake a second pizza with the remaining ingredients.

TARTE FLAMBÉE

> *Call it French pizza.* Tarte Flambée is an Alsatian specialty, a flatbread classically topped with mild fresh cheese, crème fraîche, onions, and bacon. It has become more familiar on New York menus in recent years. And it is showcased at August, a small Greenwich Village treasure that has attracted a steady clientele with a menu that trolls Europe for its varied offerings.

SERVES 6 TO 8

1 packet active dry yeast
½ teaspoon sugar
2 tablespoons extra virgin olive oil
Sea salt
2⅓ cups all-purpose flour, approximately
½ pound slab bacon, diced
4 medium onions, sliced thin
1½ cups crème fraîche
½ cup fromage blanc
3 cloves garlic, minced
¼ cup semolina flour or cornmeal

In a large bowl dissolve the yeast and sugar in ½ cup warm water. Set aside to proof for about 5 minutes. Add 1 tablespoon of the olive oil, ½ teaspoon sea salt, and ½ cup warm water. Add most of the flour, ½ cup at a time, stirring with a wooden spoon until a dough forms that leaves the sides of the bowl. Turn dough out onto a lightly floured work surface and knead for about 8 minutes, until the dough is smooth and springy, adding flour as needed to keep it from being too sticky. Shape the dough into a ball.

Brush a bowl that is about twice the size of your ball of dough with ½ tablespoon of the olive oil. Place the dough in the bowl and turn it so it becomes coated with oil on all sides. Cover it loosely and set it aside to rise until doubled, about 1 hour at room temperature, longer in the refrigerator.

Meanwhile, in a medium-large skillet, cook the bacon over medium heat until golden. Add the onions and cook, stirring, until they become lightly browned, about 10 minutes. Remove from heat and set aside.

In a bowl mix together the crème fraîche, fromage blanc, and garlic. Season with salt. Reserve.

Preheat the oven to 500 degrees. Brush a pizza pan with the remaining olive oil and dust it lightly with semolina flour or cornmeal. Set the oven rack to the lowest position.

A richly assertive Alsatian gewürztraminer with perhaps a hint of smoke on the palate

Punch the dough down, knead it briefly, then roll and stretch it to fit the pan. Spread the cream mixture over the dough, leaving about an inch of border, then scatter the bacon and onion mixture on top. Bake until the crust is lightly browned and crisp around the edges, about 15 minutes. Serve in wedges.

KASHMIRI MUSHROOM BRUSCHETTA

Indian restaurants in New York often play the game of "me too," unwilling to abandon crowd-pleasers like chicken tikka masala and tandoori lamb. But Suvir Saran and the chef, Hemant Mathur, who own Dévi, prove that more can be done. Mr. Saran, who is a chef himself, as well as a cookbook author, has created a kind of fusion cuisine that maintains Indian seasonings and flavors while breaking away from classic dishes. For example, his fried chicken is uncommonly delicious. These open-face mushroom bruschettas, seasoned with a panoply of Indian spices, are another example.

Fenugreek and garam masala are among the more exotic ingredients used in Indian cooking. Fortunately, these days, there are online sources for them (see page 258).

Smaller rounds of toasted baguette can also be used for these canapés; you will be able to make about 36.

2 tablespoons canola oil

1 teaspoon cumin seeds

3 whole small dried red chilis, crushed

2-inch piece fresh ginger, peeled and minced

1 large red onion, finely diced

1 jalapeño pepper, cored, seeded, and slivered lengthwise

Salt

¼ cup dried fenugreek leaves

2 garlic cloves, very finely chopped

1 tablespoon ground coriander

¼ teaspoon cayenne

1 pound small cremini mushrooms, trimmed and quartered

1 large tomato, cut into ½-inch pieces

2 tablespoons tomato paste

¼ cup plus 2 tablespoons chopped fresh cilantro

¼ teaspoon garam masala

16 slices country bread, both sides brushed with olive oil and toasted

Heat the oil over medium-high heat in a large skillet, add the cumin seeds and chilis, and cook, stirring, until the cumin turns light brown, 1 to 2 minutes. Add the ginger and cook, stirring, about 30 seconds. Add the onion, jalapeño, and ½ teaspoon salt and cook, stirring often, until the onion softens and begins to brown around the edges, about 5 minutes. Add the fenugreek leaves and cook for another 2 minutes.

Reduce the heat to low. Add the garlic, coriander, and cayenne and cook, stirring, for 1 minute. Add the mushrooms and turn the heat back up to medium-high. Cook, stirring occasionally, until the mushrooms are mostly cooked through, about 5 minutes.

Add the tomato, tomato paste, ½ cup water, and ¼ cup of the cilantro. Bring to a simmer and cook, stirring often, until the sauce thickens around the mushrooms, about 5 minutes. Add the garam masala and cook for a minute. Add salt to taste. Spoon the mixture onto the toasted bread, cut each slice in half, sprinkle with the remaining cilantro, and serve.

Austrian wines, either a grüner veltliner white from the Kamptal region or a blaufränisch red

CHICKEN LIVER CROSTINI

TRATTORIA DELL'ARTE

A huge antipasti display, copious portions, and decor that is at once rustic Italian and whimsical—with its artistic studies of noses and other body parts that seem to reflect The Art Students League down the street—all set Trattoria dell'Arte apart. Shelly Fireman, who owns this restaurant and several others nearby—including Brooklyn Diner USA, Redeye Grill, and Shelly's New York, as well as Fiorello's, another Italian fantasy, across from Lincoln Center—does not mind a touch of whimsy in his places. Consider the noses.

SERVES 4

¾ pound chicken livers,
    well trimmed and cut into
    1-inch pieces
Salt and freshly ground black pepper
4 (¾-inch-thick) slices Tuscan
    bread or other crusty bread
1 garlic clove, cut in half
    lengthwise
3 tablespoons extra virgin olive oil
¼ cup balsamic vinegar, at least
    10 years old

> The secret to this dish is to make sure the livers are seared on the outside, pink in the middle, and well glazed with the balsamic reduction. It is best to accomplish this by cooking one portion at a time, restaurant-style. At home, though, cooking them all at once is easier and still gives a good result.

Dry the livers on several sheets of paper towel. Season with salt and pepper.

Toast the bread slices, rub them with the garlic halves, and drizzle them with 1 tablespoon of the olive oil. Cut each slice in thirds. Arrange the bread on a warm serving plate and set aside. Heat the remaining oil in a large nonstick skillet. When the oil is very hot, add the livers, being careful not to crowd them. If all the pieces don't fit in the skillet, cook them in two batches. Sear the livers on one side, then turn and sear the other side, reduce heat to medium, and continue cooking 3 to 5 minutes for each side. The livers should still be pink inside. Add the vinegar and turn the livers in the pan juices to baste. Spoon the livers and warm sauce over the toast slices, re-season with salt and pepper, and serve.

 A robust Chianti

FRIED COD SANDWICH

PEARL OYSTER BAR

There are all sorts of oyster bars in New York, but Pearl Oyster Bar is an uncommon example; a little taste of New England in Greenwich Village. In fact, it's more about beachside fried clams, lobster rolls, and crab cakes than just oysters. Rebecca Charles, the owner, grew up summering in Kennebunkport on the coast of Maine, and began her career at the Whistling Oyster in Ogunquit. Lobster rolls are now on dozens of Manhattan menus, and Charles can claim responsibility. But where else can you order a fried cod sandwich?

SERVES 2

2 (5- to 6-ounce) fillets of cod, haddock, flounder, or sole

1 cup milk

Salt and freshly ground black pepper

½ cup all-purpose flour

¼ cup cracker meal

¼ cup canola, peanut, or soy oil

2 ciabatta rolls, Portuguese rolls, or other flat, crusty rolls

½ cup tartar sauce

½ ripe tomato, peeled and thinly sliced

½ small red onion, thinly sliced

4 to 6 Bibb or Boston lettuce leaves

> If you use flounder or sole, it will cook faster, about 2 to 3 minutes per side.

Preheat the oven to 450 degrees.

Soak the fish in milk for 5 minutes, drain it, and lay it on a plate. Season the fish with salt and pepper. On a large plate combine the flour and cracker meal. Dredge the fish on both sides with this mixture, dusting off excess.

Heat an ovenproof skillet over high heat, add the oil and when very hot, place the fish in the pan with the whiter side down. When the crust is golden brown, after 3 to 4 minutes, flip the fillets over and place the pan in the oven for 4 to 5 minutes, to finish cooking. At this time place the rolls in the oven, to warm them for a minute or two.

Split the rolls in half horizontally with a sharp, serrated knife. Spread both halves of each roll liberally with tartar sauce. Layer the tomato, onion, and lettuce on the bottom halves and season to taste with salt and pepper. When the fish is done, place it on the bottom halves, close the sandwiches, and serve.

 Rebecca Charles admits that beer is best.

OPEN-FACE TUNA SALAD SANDWICHES

LE PAIN QUOTIDIEN

Alain Coumont started his chain of farmhouse-style bakery-cafés in Belgium, expanded it to other European countries, and finally brought his concept to New York. There are more than a dozen restaurant-shops in the city now: the original one on Madison Avenue, and others all over town. What distinguishes these places is Coumont's commitment to using as many organic ingredients as possible. His breads are made with organic flour; his salads rely on organic greens, oils, and vinegars; and even the milk for his organic coffee is organic.

SERVES 2

1 (6½-ounce) can tuna in olive oil, drained

2 tablespoons diced organic celery

2 tablespoons peeled, diced organic onion

2 teaspoons sherry vinegar

1½ tablespoons organic olive oil

2 teaspoons Dijon mustard

2 teaspoons organic mayonnaise

Salt and freshly ground black pepper

2 large slices organic wheat bread

2 tablespoons black olive paste or tapenade

½ roasted red pepper in oil

Mesclun greens and cucumber slices, for serving

European tuna in olive oil has much better flavor than white albacore tuna in water.

Use a fork to break up the tuna in a bowl. Add the celery, onion, vinegar, olive oil, mustard, and mayonnaise, and mix well. Season to taste with salt and pepper. Spread the tuna salad on each of the two slices of bread. Cut each slice into four sections. Spread a little of the olive paste on each section. Cut the roasted red pepper into 8 strips and place one on each section. Transfer the sandwiches to 2 salad plates, garnish with mesclun greens and cucumber slices, and serve.

 Organic iced tea

SEAFOOD

GRILLED FILET MIGNON OF TUNA 116

WILD KING SALMON IN SWISS CHARD WITH QUINOA 118

LEMONGRASS-CRUSTED SWORDFISH
WITH THAI PEANUT SAUCE 120

HERB-ROASTED SALMON WITH HORSERADISH 122

KAKAVIA, GREEK FISHERMAN'S STEW 123

STEAMED HALIBUT WITH BLACK BEAN SAUCE 124

STRIPED BASS WITH RED WINE SAUCE AND SAGE 126

BLACK COD WITH MISO 128

SPICY SHELLFISH YIOUVESTI 130

CODFISH WITH SWEET GARLIC SAUCE
AND CHORIZO ESSENCE 132

SHRIMP WITH MANGO 135

BUTTER-POACHED LOBSTER 136

LOBSTER FRA DIAVOLO 138

GRILLED FILET MIGNON OF TUNA
UNION SQUARE CAFE

When Danny Meyer opened Union Square Cafe in 1985, the New York restaurant scene was vastly different. The dining public was just starting to be seduced by the allure of new American kitchens and young American chefs; the chefs themselves were beginning to notice the potential that local farmers represented. Union Square Cafe's chef, French-trained Michael Romano, was in the vanguard of those who took advantage of what the burgeoning nearby Greenmarket had to offer. At lunch, it's a downtown version of the Grill Room at The Four Seasons, with publishing moguls, authors, and agents filling the tables. Dinner is for New Yorkers and visitors with the foresight to reserve well in advance, or who do not mind digging into the lusty Italianate food with a glass of wine at the bar. Danny Meyer has added other nearby restaurants to his portfolio: Eleven Madison Park, Tabla, Gramercy Tavern, Blue Smoke, and the wildly popular hot dog stand, Shake Shack.

SERVES 4 TO 6

2 cups teriyaki sauce

½ cup dry sherry

4 tablespoons minced fresh ginger

½ cup minced scallions

2 garlic cloves, thinly sliced

½ teaspoon cayenne

2 teaspoons freshly ground black
    pepper

Juice of 2 lemons, about ¼ cup

4 yellowfin tuna steaks, each about
    8 ounces and cut 2½ to 3 inches
    thick

2 tablespoons extra virgin olive oil

¼ cup Japanese pickled ginger,
    drained

Most fish markets do not cut their tuna steaks thicker than about 1½ to 2 inches. It will probably be necessary for you to place a special order for the tuna. If you can get only thinner steaks, the tuna can be cut in chunks, marinated, strung on skewers, and grilled like kebabs.

Combine the teriyaki sauce, sherry, fresh ginger, scallions, garlic, cayenne, black pepper, and lemon juice in a bowl large enough to hold the tuna. Cut each tuna steak vertically in three equal pieces. Place the tuna in the marinade, cover the bowl, and let it sit in the refrigerator for 3 hours. Turn the tuna every hour.

A half hour before serving, remove the tuna from the refrigerator, drain off the marinade, and put the tuna on a platter. Preheat a grill or broiler. You can also use a heavy-duty stove-top grill pan, but it will not need to be pre-heated for more than 10 minutes.

Brush the tuna with olive oil. Grill or broil the tuna a minute or two on each of its 6 sides, so the outside is charred but the center is barely warm and still quite rare. Top each piece of tuna with a little of the pickled ginger and serve at once.

A Cornas from the Rhône, a tokay pinot gris from Alsace, or chilled beer

WILD KING SALMON IN SWISS CHARD WITH QUINOA

RIVER CAFÉ

The Brooklyn waterfront has perhaps the best views of Lower Manhattan, and that's what makes the River Café so magical. It's literally right at the edge of the East River, and were it any closer to the Brooklyn Bridge, it would be under it. But the restaurant, owned by Buzzy O'Keeffe—who also master-minded places like the Water Club, on the Manhattan side of the river in Midtown, and Pershing Square, across from Grand Central Terminal—has been an incubator for some of the city's best chefs, including Larry Forgione, Charles Palmer, David Burke, and Rick Laakkonen.

SERVES 6

1 bunch red Swiss chard, heavy stems removed

6 tablespoons unsalted butter

1 celery stalk, finely diced

2 carrots, peeled and finely diced

2 leeks, white part only, well-rinsed, finely diced

1½ cups quinoa

3 cups hot chicken stock

3 (10- to 12-ounce) king salmon steaks

2 tablespoons finely minced preserved lemon (sold in Middle Eastern food shops)

1 shallot, peeled and minced

½ teaspoon ground star anise or Chinese five-spice powder

1 cup dry red wine

2 cups tawny port

Salt and freshly ground black pepper

½ teaspoon lemon juice

Bring a large pot of water to a boil. Place several layers of paper towels nearby on your countertop. Place a Swiss chard leaf in the water, scoop it out as soon as it wilts, and lay it flat on the towel. Repeat with the remaining Swiss chard leaves. Roll the Swiss chard leaves in the paper towels and set aside.

Heat 1½ tablespoons of the butter in a heavy 3-quart saucepan. Add the celery, carrots, and leeks, and sauté over medium-low heat until translucent. Add the quinoa, stir it for a few minutes, then gradually add the chicken stock. Cover, lower the heat, and cook until the quinoa is tender, about 15 minutes. Remove from the heat and keep covered. The quinoa can be prepared in advance and reheated just before serving.

Remove the skin from the salmon steaks, cut each steak in half, and remove the bones. This will give you 6 uniform fillets. Spread one side of each piece of salmon with some of the preserved lemon. Then wrap each piece of salmon in a Swiss chard leaf, enclosing it completely as in an enve-lope. You may have to use more than one leaf for each piece

Purchase wild king salmon from the Pacific Northwest or Alaska. It is a native fish, not farm-raised, and has better flavor and texture.

of fish. Place 2 wrapped fish fillets in a Ziploc sandwich bag and seal the bag. Repeat with the remaining fillets. Refrigerate until about 15 to 20 minutes before serving.

Heat ½ tablespoon of the butter in a small saucepan. Add the shallot and star anise and sauté until tender. Add the wine and port, and boil until reduced to about 1 cup. Keeping the wine mixture at a bare simmer, whisk in the remaining 4 tablespoons of butter, bit by bit, until the sauce is thickened. Season to taste with salt and pepper. Add the lemon juice. Keep warm.

Remove the fish from the refrigerator. Bring about 1 inch of water to a boil in a pot or deep covered frying pan large enough to hold the bags of fish in one flat layer. Place a steamer over the boiling water. Place the fish, still sealed in the plastic bags, in the steamer, cover the pot, and cook for about 8 minutes. Remove the fish from steamer and allow to rest 5 minutes. While the fish is resting, reheat the quinoa.

Divide the quinoa among 6 warm dinner plates. Carefully open the plastic bags and place a wrapped fish fillet alongside the quinoa. Drizzle the warm wine sauce over the fish and around the quinoa, and serve.

Alsatian Riesling, another full-bodied dry riesling, Pinot Noir from Oregon, or a light red Burgundy

LEMONGRASS-CRUSTED SWORDFISH WITH THAI PEANUT SAUCE

ROY'S NEW YORK

Roy Yamaguchi, who brought the luau tastes of Hawaii to New York, was born in Japan, trained at the Culinary Institute of America in Hyde Park, New York, and worked in Los Angeles before settling in Honolulu. From there he created his Roy's empire, with several places in Hawaii, outposts in Tokyo and Guam, and restaurants in California and Manhattan. His cooking is brash and well-spiced, and balances sweet and sour flavors. Seafood is his specialty. This dish is made in Hawaii with a fish called shutome, but swordfish is a fine substitute.

Most of the specialized ingredients are sold in Asian stores.

The sauce can be made in advance and reheated when the fish is ready to serve.

1 cup unsweetened coconut milk

⅓ cup packed light brown sugar

⅓ cup soy sauce

1 tablespoon *nam pla* (Thai fish sauce)

2 teaspoons rice vinegar

1 tablespoon lemon juice

2 teaspoons Thai *Masaman* curry paste, or 2 teaspoons curry powder

5 tablespoons creamy peanut butter

¼ cup minced sweet onion such as Maui

2 tablespoons minced cilantro leaves

1 kaffir lime leaf, minced, or 1 teaspoon grated lime zest

2 tablespoons minced fresh basil leaves, preferably Thai opal

1½ tablespoons minced garlic

1½ tablespoons minced fresh ginger

2 tablespoons minced lemongrass bulb

1 tablespoon minced shallots

1 teaspoon *shichimi* (Japanese pepper), or ½ teaspoon each cayenne and black pepper

3 tablespoons canola oil

1½ pounds swordfish steaks, skinned, cut into 4 portions

Salt

Japanese pickled ginger and cilantro sprigs, for garnish

Though this recipe requires what looks like a thousand ingredients, it is actually very simple to prepare.

For the sauce, whisk together in a small saucepan the coconut milk, brown sugar, soy sauce, fish sauce, rice vinegar, lemon juice, curry, peanut butter, onion, cilantro, kaffir lime leaf, basil, and ½ tablespoon each of the garlic and ginger. Bring to a boil, reduce the heat, and simmer about 30 minutes.

Meanwhile, mix the remaining tablespoon each of garlic and ginger with the lemongrass, shallots, and *shichimi*. Beat in the oil. You can do this in a food processor. Season the fish with salt. Spread the lemongrass mixture on one side of each piece of the fish.

Heat a large nonstick skillet over medium-high heat. Place the pieces of fish in it, crusted side down, and sauté until golden, about 3 minutes. Use a spatula to carefully turn the fish so as not to lose any of the crust. Continue cooking until the fish is just cooked through, another 5 minutes or so.

While the fish is cooking, reheat the sauce, thinning it with a splash of water if necessary.

Place the fish on a serving dish, garnish with pickled ginger and cilantro, and serve with the sauce alongside.

Passion fruit margaritas made with silver tequila, passion fruit puree, fresh lime juice, and simple syrup. Beer or fruity white wine are good alternatives.

HERB-ROASTED SALMON WITH HORSERADISH

BEACON

A wood-burning oven is a coveted accessory in New York's restaurant kitchens. Often, its use is limited to pizza. But at Beacon the chef, Waldy Malouf, relies on it for cooking everything from the first-course oysters to pears for dessert. The restaurant is a spacious room with a mezzanine. But the focus is the hearth, open to view, where the chefs use long-handled peels to move sizzling dishes in and out of the roaring oven, and the most prized table is right in front of it.

SERVES 4

2 tablespoons soft white bread crumbs

5 tablespoons prepared horseradish

Freshly ground white pepper

5 tablespoons extra virgin olive oil

2½ tablespoons minced fresh basil

2½ tablespoons minced fresh tarragon

2½ tablespoons minced fresh dill

1½ tablespoons minced fresh mint

Salt

1¼ pounds fresh salmon fillet, skinned and cut into 8 equal pieces

Place the bread crumbs and 3 tablespoons of the horseradish in a mortar and mix well. Season with pepper. Add 3 tablespoons of the oil in a thin stream, beating constantly. Thin the sauce with a tablespoon or two of water so it is slightly thinner than mayonnaise. Set aside.

Preheat the oven to 500 degrees.

Mix 1 tablespoon of the oil with the remaining horseradish. Mix in 2 tablespoons each of the basil, tarragon, and dill, and 1 tablespoon of the mint. Season with salt and pepper. Use a little of the remaining oil to grease a baking dish that will hold the fish in a single layer. Season the fish with salt and pepper and arrange in the pan skinned side down. Spoon the horseradish-herb mixture on top of each piece of the fish, place the pan in the oven, and bake 6 to 8 minutes, until the fish is not quite cooked through.

Remove from the oven and place 2 pieces of fish on each of 4 plates. Spoon some of the horseradish-bread sauce around each portion, sprinkle with some of the remaining herbs and a few drops of the remaining oil, and serve.

When wild Pacific salmon from Alaska or Washington is in season, it is a better choice for both flavor and the environment than farm-raised Atlantic salmon.

An Oregon pinot gris, or a light red Burgundy

KAKAVIA, GREEK FISHERMAN'S STEW

ESTIATORIO MILOS

Estiatorio Milos, the New York branch of a popular Montreal restaurant, has generated a trend. The estiatorio, or market-style Greek fish restaurant, did not exist in New York before Milos opened. And now it has spawned a handful of imitators which, like the original, specialize in serving fresh fish, by the pound. When diners are seated, the house's own olive oil is poured over crushed herbs as a dip for crusty country bread, then the market choices are described.

SERVES 6

2 large onions, peeled and cut into chunks

2 pounds Yukon gold potatoes, peeled and cut into chunks

3 pounds assorted fish fillets and steaks, such as striped bass, sea bass, grouper, cod, monkfish

1 cup best-quality extra virgin olive oil

1 tablespoon coarse sea salt

Freshly ground black pepper

18 (2-inch) chunks country bread, toasted

Juice of ½ lemon (about 1 tablespoon)

12 sprigs flat-leaf parsley

Ideally, you'll want to use at least three kinds of fish in this stew. In Greece the choices would include a rockfish like rascasse, the fish that is essential to bouillabaisse. But any firm, chunky, lean fish works.

You'll need a deep 6-quart pot to assemble this hearty, amazingly simple fisherman's stew. Put the onions in the bottom of the pot. Cover the onions with the potato chunks. Then add the fish, all of which should be in fairly large pieces. Pour ½ cup of the good olive oil—emphasis on the good, please—over it all.

Measure out 3 cups of water and dissolve the sea salt in it; add some pepper and pour it into the pot. Cover the pot and put it on high heat. Once it comes to a boil, lower the heat just a bit and let it cook 12 minutes.

While the kakavia bubbles away, brush the bread cubes with about ¼ cup of the remaining olive oil.

After the 12 minutes are up, remove the pot from the heat and carefully ladle the fish and vegetables out of the pot, into 6 generous soup plates or bowls. Add the lemon juice to the pot. The broth now should be flavorful and slightly thickened from the potatoes and the emulsified olive oil— that's what happens when it boils: it's the bouillabaisse principle. Bring the broth back to the simmer, and ladle it over the fish and vegetables. Drizzle on the rest of the olive oil, top each portion with the bread cubes and parsley, and serve at once.

 White Greek wine, especially Laoutari.

STEAMED HALIBUT WITH
BLACK BEAN SAUCE

MORIMOTO

Morimoto is an import from Philadelphia to New York's meatpacking district, and it does not shrink from grandeur. This Japanese restaurant's two levels, with different areas, including sushi bars, create an atmosphere of bustling activity that is modulated by some glass-enclosed enclaves with tables for four. It is the first restaurant that the celebrated Japanese architect Tadao Ando designed, and among its notable features is a rippling, pleated ceiling. Masaharu Morimoto, the chef, first attracted attention at Nobu, before heading to Philadelphia for a partnership with Stephen Starr. His New York menu is as wide-ranging as the place itself, with unusual main dishes and grilled items to supplement a vast array of sushi choices.

SERVES 4

1 tablespoon fermented black beans

2 tablespoons plus 1 cup sake

1½ teaspoons Chinese oyster sauce

1½ teaspoons soy sauce

½ teaspoon sugar

1 small clove garlic, finely minced

1½ pounds halibut fillets, in 4 equal
   pieces

2 tablespoons peanut oil

¼ cup finely slivered fresh ginger

2 scallions, all but about an inch of
   green trimmed, finely slivered

1 tablespoon nuoc mam
   (Vietnamese fish sauce)

4 fresh cilantro sprigs

Crush the black beans in a mortar or with the flat side of a cleaver. Mix them in a small bowl with the 2 tablespoons sake, the oyster sauce, soy sauce, sugar, and garlic.

Place the halibut in a ceramic or glass dish and coat the pieces with the black bean mixture.

Heat the oil in a small skillet and fry the ginger and scallions until they are crispy. Drain on paper towels.

Shortly before serving, place the remaining cup of sake in the bottom of a steamer. Place the coated fish in the steamer, cover, and steam until just cooked through, about 5 minutes. Place each portion of fish in a shallow soup plate and top with the fried ginger and scallions. Strain the sake from the steamer, stir in the fish sauce, and spoon some of this broth around the fish. Garnish each portion with a sprig of cilantro and serve at once.

 Chilled daiginjo sake is best.

STRIPED BASS WITH RED WINE SAUCE AND SAGE

CHANTERELLE

Chanterelle is a pioneer, one of the first fine restaurants to open in SoHo. It has moved since then, conquering new territory in TriBeCa. The dining room is airy and understated, deriving its elegance from stunning sprays of flowers, a few carefully chosen antique pieces, and magnificent chandeliers. David Waltuck, the chef who owns Chanterelle with his wife, Karen, is celebrated for his finely crafted imaginative French-accented American food.

3 tablespoons fresh sage leaves

½ teaspoon chopped garlic

Juice of ½ lemon (about 1 tablespoon)

4 tablespoons soft unsalted butter

Salt and freshly ground black pepper

1½ pounds wild striped bass fillets with skin, in 4 equal portions

3 tablespoons red wine vinegar

3 tablespoons minced shallots

1 cup dry red wine

2 tablespoons *glace de viande* (veal glaze)

8 tablespoons (1 stick) cold unsalted butter, diced

⅓ cup Wondra or all-purpose flour

3 tablespoons extra virgin olive oil

Farm-raised striped bass is more easily obtained than Atlantic wild striped bass, but there is no comparison. The wild fish is meatier and more muscular. Black sea bass and even Pacific king salmon can be substituted.

In this recipe the sage butter actually melts away when the fish is seared but the flavor of sage and butter permeate the fish and the skin becomes extremely crisp.

Place the sage, garlic, lemon juice, and soft butter in a small food processor or in a mortar. Process or pound until smooth. Season with salt and pepper.

Use a sharp knife to lift the skin off the fish, leaving it attached at one edge. Spread the sage butter on the fish, and replace the flap of skin to enclose the butter. Refrigerate until just before cooking.

Place the vinegar and shallots in a small saucepan. Cook until shallots are translucent and vinegar just films the bottom of the pan. Add the wine, cook until reduced to about ¼ cup. Stir in veal glaze, then lower heat. Whisk in the cold butter bit by bit, whisking constantly, until the sauce has thickened. Season to taste with salt and pepper. Cover, set aside, and keep warm.

Fifteen to 20 minutes before serving, dust the fish fillets with the flour and shake off any excess. In a large sauté pan, heat the olive oil until it's nearly smoking. Add the fish, skin side down, and sear until lightly browned. Turn and sear on the second side until cooked through. Count on close to 10 minutes total cooking time. Transfer the fish portions to individual dinner plates, skin side up. Gently reheat the red wine sauce, spoon around the fish, and serve.

Vosne-Romanée Les Malconsorts or another full-bodied red Burgundy

BLACK COD WITH MISO

NOBU

It was inevitable that Nobu Matsuhisa, who opened Matsuhisa in Los Angeles in 1987 to rave reviews, would wind up in New York. Even without having Robert De Niro as a regular at the sushi bar in his Los Angeles spot, a chef whose food is as original as Nobu's would be attracted to New York. Here the design by David Rockwell is stunning, with bare wood and a wall of sea pebbles. Nobu's classic Japanese training fused with a seven-year stint in Lima, Peru, to shape his cuisine. Sashimi meets ceviche. Nobu regulars let the chef decide the menu. But inevitably, they'll want a taste of his famous, often-imitated Black Cod with Miso. Although seats are hard to secure, reservations are not necessary at the sushi bar. At the equally innovative spin-off, Next Door Nobu, it's first-come, first-served. There is another Nobu in midtown.

SERVES 4

¼ cup sake

¾ cup mirin

2 cups white miso paste

1¼ cups sugar

4 black cod (sablefish) fillets with skin, each about 8 ounces

Japanese pickled ginger, for garnish

Robert De Niro's favorite drink with this dish is chilled sake.

The glaze is also delicious with salmon, tuna, and even beef fillets. But then you may want to reduce the baking time, so the center of the fish or meat is medium rare.

Bring the sake and mirin to a boil in a medium saucepan over high heat. Boil 20 seconds. Reduce heat to low and stir in miso paste with a wooden spoon. When miso has dissolved, increase the heat to medium and stir in the sugar. Cook, stirring constantly, until the sugar dissolves. Remove from heat and cool to room temperature. This mixture is the key to the recipe.

Pat the fish dry with paper towel. Place in a nonreactive dish, pour on the cooled miso mixture, and turn the fish to coat it completely. Cover tightly with plastic wrap and refrigerate 2 to 3 days. The marinating is another key.

Preheat the oven to 400 degrees. Preheat a grill, grill pan, or broiler.

Remove the fish from the marinade, lightly wiping off any excess. Place the fish on the grill or under the broiler with the skin toward the heat, and sear until the skin is just browned. Transfer to a baking dish, skin side up, and bake about 10 minutes, until just cooked through.

Arrange on dinner plates and garnish with ginger.

SPICY SHELLFISH YIOUVESTI

There is no doubt that Anthos in Midtown is a rarity, a Greek restaurant where the food is rooted in tradition yet, in the hands of the chef and co-owner, Michael Psilakis, highly inventive. Psilakis does not hesitate to borrow from elsewhere in the Mediterranean. Using espelette pepper, a Basque seasoning, in this seafood stew, is one example. The restaurant, decorated in sleekly modern upscale style, offers tasting menus with dishes complemented by wines from a deep list of Greek bottles.

2 lobsters, 1 pound each

6 cups fish stock

½ teaspoon saffron threads

Salt

Espelette pepper or cayenne

1 cup orzo

¼ cup extra virgin olive oil

2 shallots, sliced

1 large clove garlic, sliced

¼ teaspoon smoked paprika

2 tablespoons sherry vinegar

8 mahogany or littleneck clams, scrubbed

12 cockles, scrubbed

12 mussels, scrubbed

4 jumbo shrimp in shells, split lengthwise

½ teaspoon dried Greek oregano

2 teaspoons Thai or Vietnamese fish sauce

1 tablespoon lemon juice

1 teaspoon minced fresh dill

1 teaspoon minced flat-leaf parsley

1 teaspoon minced fresh mint

Crusty bread, for serving

> Feel free to improvise when you buy the seafood for this stew—the more variety the better. At Anthos, they might add razor clams, whelks, and crayfish. You can also adjust the quantities, depending on what you prefer. Just be sure to have bowls for discarded shells on the table.

Bring a pot of water large enough to hold the lobsters to a boil. Add the lobsters, cook 3 minutes, then drain. (Alternatively, lobsters can be purchased already cooked.) When the lobsters are cool enough to handle, remove the claws and tails. Reserve the knuckles for another use. Use kitchen shears to split the tails, still in their shells, in half. Remove the claw meat from the shells.

Place the stock in a 3-quart saucepan, Add half of the saffron, along with salt and espelette or cayenne to taste, and bring to a simmer. Add the orzo, cook 5 minutes, then strain it through a sieve, reserving both the orzo and the stock.

In a 6-quart casserole, warm 2 tablespoons of the oil over medium heat. Add the shallots, garlic, and paprika. Sauté until the shallots are soft, season with espelette or cayenne, then stir in the vinegar. Add 1 cup of the reserved stock and the clams, cockles, and mussels. Cover and cook until the shellfish open, about 8 minutes. Remove the shellfish to a large bowl, draining them well. Discard any that are unopened. Cover to keep warm.

To the stock in the casserole, add the orzo, shrimp, remaining saffron, oregano, fish sauce, and lemon juice. Cook until the shrimp just turn pink. Taste the broth for seasoning and add salt and espelette or cayenne as needed. Add the clams, cockles, mussels, and lobster pieces. Simmer a few minutes to heat the ingredients, then dust with dill, parsley, and mint.

Transfer the stew to a large, warm tureen or serving bowl, or to individual bowls, drizzle on the remaining olive oil, and serve with plenty of crusty bread.

 An aromatic malagousia white from Epanomi, Greece, or a smoky agiorghitiko red from Nemea

CODFISH WITH SWEET GARLIC SAUCE AND CHORIZO ESSENCE

LE BERNARDIN

One month after Le Bernardin opened in 1986, it was acknowledged to be the best seafood restaurant in the city, if not the country. Its reputation has never tarnished. The original chef and owner, Gilbert Le Coze, and his sister and partner, Maguy Le Coze, who transplanted their Paris restaurant to grand quarters in Midtown, did not set about to change the way America eats fish, but their approach, undercooking some varieties ever so slightly and preparing others, like salmon, closer to rare, accomplished just that. Because pristine freshness was so paramount, Gilbert Le Coze became a denizen of the Fulton Fish Market. He led the way so that the freshness he demanded has become much easier to obtain. After his sudden death from a heart attack, he was succeeded as chef and partner by Eric Ripert, who maintains Le Bernardin's high standards, and who has broadened the scope of the menu, with some Asian and Spanish flavors.

SERVES 6

3 heads garlic
½ cup extra virgin olive oil
3 medium ripe tomatoes
4 fresh thyme sprigs
1 link chorizo sausage, preferably
    Spanish
1 cup chicken stock
½ cup heavy cream
Sea salt and freshly ground white
    pepper
2 tablespoons canola or grapeseed oil
6 (6-ounce) fillets fresh cod, skinned
Espelette pepper or Spanish hot
    paprika to taste
12 thin slices baguette, toasted
Chervil sprigs, for garnish

Preheat the oven to 200 degrees.

Slice off the top ½ inch of the garlic heads. Place the garlic on a sheet of heavy-duty aluminum foil, drizzle with ¼ cup of the olive oil, wrap tightly, and place on a baking sheet lined with parchment. Core the tomatoes and cut each in 6 wedges. Place on the parchment-lined baking sheet, and drizzle with remaining ¼ cup olive oil. Place the thyme sprigs on top of the tomatoes and place baking sheet in the oven for 2½ hours.

Meanwhile, peel the chorizo and slice it thin. Place in a small saucepan and cook over medium heat until sausage is browned and fat is rendered. Off heat carefully add 1 cup water—it may spatter—and cook until the liquid is reduced by half. Strain through a fine sieve, pressing the chorizo to extract as much liquid as possible. Return the liquid to the saucepan and discard the chorizo slices.

The best way to tell when fish is perfectly cooked is the skewer test. Take a thin metal skewer, like a turkey lacer, and insert it in the center of the fish at an angle. Leave it in for 5 seconds, then touch the skewer to your chin, just below your lower lip. If it is just warm, most fish such as cod or halibut will be perfectly done. If you want your fish rare, the skewer should be almost cool. You should also feel how the skewer slides into the fish. It should meet no resistance.

A viognier from the Rhône valley

When the garlic is tender and the tomatoes are cooked, remove them from the oven. Set the tomatoes aside. Using the back of a knife, press out the cloves from the heads of garlic. Reserve 6 cloves. Place the remaining cloves in a blender with ½ cup of the chicken stock. Puree, then pass through a fine sieve into a clean saucepan. Stir in the remaining chicken stock and the cream. Bring to a simmer and cook about 5 minutes, until slightly thickened. Season to taste with salt and pepper. Set aside. (All this preparation can be done hours in advance.)

If necessary, preheat the oven again to 200 degrees. Place the tomato pieces and the 6 reserved garlic cloves in the oven to warm.

Heat the canola oil in one large or two medium skillets until very hot. Dry the cod, season with salt and pepper, and place in the skillet presentation side down (that is, the whiter side that did not have the skin). Cook about 5 minutes, until golden. Flip and cook the other side until just done, another 3 to 5 minutes. Remove from the heat and transfer to 6 soup plates. Reheat the garlic sauce and spoon around fish. Place the tomato pieces around fish. Slice each reserved garlic clove into 3 slivers, and scatter over the tomatoes. Reheat chorizo essence and drizzle about a teaspoon on each portion. Dust with espelette pepper, place the baguette slices alongside the fish, garnish with chervil, and serve.

SHRIMP WITH MANGO

At this sprawling restaurant, with Chinese décor that's just this side of kitsch—lacquer screens, tasseled hanging lanterns, foo dogs, and a basin of koi fish—you will see how very good Chinese food can be. The chef, Joe Ng, whose specialty is dim sum (and his dumplings are terrific), also knows his way around a stir-fry wok and a barbecue oven. These shrimp with mango are a prime example of how light and tasty his creations can be.

SERVES 4

½ pound medium shrimp, peeled and deveined

1 large egg white

1 tablespoon potato starch or cornstarch

Salt and freshly ground white pepper

3 red radishes, trimmed and sliced thin

1¼ pounds sugar snap peas, ends and strings removed

1 ripe mango, peeled, pitted, and cut in ½-inch dice

2-inch piece fresh ginger, peeled and sliced thin

1 bunch scallions, trimmed, white part only, halved lengthwise

1 large clove garlic, finely chopped

¼ cup peanut or soybean oil

½ cup Chinese Shaoxing rice wine

½ teaspoon sugar

Steamed rice, for serving

Place the shrimp in a bowl. Beat the egg white until lightly frothed, fold in ¼ teaspoon of the starch, ½ teaspoon salt, and a few turns of fresh pepper. Pour this mixture over the shrimp, toss to coat them, and set aside.

Place the radishes, sugar snap peas, mango, ginger, scallions, and garlic in a bowl. Toss.

In a small dish, dissolve the remaining starch in 3 tablespoons water. Set aside.

Heat a wok or skillet over high heat. Add 3 tablespoons of the oil. When it is very hot, add the shrimp. Stir-fry until they are just turning pink. Remove them to a dish. Discard the oil in the wok and scrape the pan clean. Replace the wok over medium-high heat, add the remaining oil, and stir-fry the vegetables and mango about 2 minutes, until the snow peas are cooked but still crunchy and bright. Add the rice wine, return the shrimp to the wok, sprinkle with sugar and more white pepper, and heat through, stirring. Drizzle the dissolved starch into the pan and stir-fry, tossing, until the sauce has thickened. Serve at once with steamed rice.

A dry but fruity Alsatian riesling or gewürztraminer

There is a new gadget that can be pressed down on a mango to remove the pit easily.

BUTTER-POACHED LOBSTER

PER SE

Thomas Keller first made his mark in New York at Rakel, at the western edge of Greenwich Village. Then this French-trained chef moved to California, where he opened the acclaimed French Laundry in Yountville. In 2004, with the debut of the elegant Per Se in the Time Warner Center, Mr. Keller returned to New York. His food is singularly inventive and finely wrought. One dish that has been his signature but which other chefs have not hesitated to copy, often without attribution, is this lobster poached in butter, a preparation at once delicate and luscious. It is usually on his menus, though the garnishes may change from time to time and season to season. His most recent interpretation requires preparing the lobster "sous-vide," a vacuum technique that few home cooks have mastered, so this recipe is something of a throwback to the original version.

SERVES 4

2 live lobsters, each 1½ pounds
White vinegar
1½ cups cabernet sauvignon
1 carrot, diced
1 small shallot, sliced
1 small onion, sliced
3 ounces white mushrooms, sliced
1 bay leaf
1 fresh thyme sprig
2 cups rich veal stock
2 tablespoons canola oil
8 white pearl onions, blanched and peeled
8 red pearl onions, blanched and peeled
4 hen-of-the-woods or oyster mushroom clusters
Sea salt

Place the lobsters in a container with a tight-fitting lid. Cover them with cold water. Remove the lobsters and measure the water. Pour the water into a large pot and add 1 tablespoon vinegar for every quart of water. Bring to a boil.

Return the lobsters to the container with the lid and pour the hot water over them. Cover and steep for 3 minutes. Remove the lobsters. Reserve the water in the container. Pull off the lobster claws and knuckles and return them to the container of water for 5 minutes. Reserve the tails and discard the bodies.

Snip through the bottom of the tail shells with shears. Remove the meat. Reserve the shells. Cut the tail meat in half lengthwise. Place the meat on a platter lined with paper towel, cover with plastic wrap and refrigerate. Remove the claws from the water and extract the meat from the shells. Remove the meat from the knuckle joints. Place the claw and knuckle meat on the platter with the tails.

2 sticks plus 6 tablespoons
   (11 ounces) unsalted butter,
   at room temperature, in pieces
Freshly ground black pepper
Fresh chervil sprigs for garnish

The method for the initial cooking of the lobsters in this recipe is extremely effective and keeps the meat very tender.

The emulsified butter used for poaching the lobster meat can be strained and chilled in the refrigerator. Discard any watery liquid that results, and freeze the rest to use for sautéing and flavoring seafood.

Place the wine in a saucepan. Add the carrot, shallot, onion, white mushrooms, bay leaf, and thyme. Bring to a boil. Use a match to ignite and burn off the alcohol. Add the tail, claw, and knuckle shells. Set aside to marinate at least 4 hours.

Remove the shells from the wine mixture. Cook the wine and vegetables on medium-high until the liquid has nearly evaporated and barely films the bottom of the pan. Add the veal stock. Cook until the liquid has reduced to barely 1 cup. Strain and return the sauce to a small saucepan and set aside.

Heat the canola oil in a skillet. Add the pearl onions and cook briefly until glazed. Remove from the pan and set aside. Add the mushrooms, sprinkle with salt, and cook, turning to brown them on all sides, about 5 minutes. Drain the mushrooms on paper towels and keep warm.

Remove the lobster meat from the refrigerator. Place 2 tablespoons of water in a saucepan. Bring to a boil then reduce the heat to very low and whisk in the butter bit by bit. Place the lobster pieces in a sauté pan that will hold them snugly in a single layer. Pour the butter mixture over them. Place the pan on very low heat and cook 5 to 6 minutes, until the lobster is heated through. Set aside. Reheat the cabernet sauce on low.

To serve, spoon some of the cabernet sauce onto each plate. Remove the lobster from the butter, draining it well, and arrange the lobster meat on top of the sauce. Place the sautéed mushrooms and onions around the lobster, sprinkle with a little sea salt and black pepper, and garnish with chervil sprigs.

James Hayes, a wine director, suggests a light red, a pinot noir like a soft Gévrey-Chambertin.

LOBSTER FRA DIAVOLO

PATSY'S

There is no question that Lobster Fra Diavolo may be a century old and has long been a favorite in Italian neighborhoods in Manhattan and Boston. Some food historians contend that this combination of lobster, spicy tomato sauce, and pasta is about as Italian as spaghetti and meatballs or veal parmesan—in other words, not. Others say it is authentically Italian and was brought here by immigrants from Naples. Whichever is true, this dish is popular at Patsy's near Carnegie Hall, once one of Frank Sinatra's favorite hangouts and in business for nearly 60 years.

4 pounds ripe plum tomatoes

¼ cup extra virgin olive oil

1 medium onion, peeled and minced

4 garlic cloves, peeled and minced

2 teaspoons red pepper flakes,
  or to taste

Salt and freshly ground black
  pepper

2 tablespoons tomato paste

¼ cup finely chopped fresh basil
  leaves

1 tablespoon chopped flat-leaf
  parsley leaves

2 (1½- to 2-pound) lobsters,
  split lengthwise

½ pound dried linguine

 The restaurant bottles and sells
its fra diavolo sauce. There's a
shortcut for you.

Use a sharp paring knife to cut a small X in the end of each tomato. Bring a large pot of water to a boil and drop in about 12 of the tomatoes, cook about a minute, then use a slotted spoon to transfer them to a bowl of ice water. Repeat with the remaining tomatoes. Core and peel the tomatoes. Chop them by hand or pulse them briefly in a food processor.

In a large saucepan, heat 2 tablespoons of the oil. Add the onion and garlic and cook until softened. Add the tomatoes with their juices and bring to a simmer. Cover and cook about 30 minutes, stirring from time to time. Add the pepper flakes and cook 20 minutes more. Season with salt and pepper, and add the tomato paste, basil, and parsley. Simmer a few minutes longer, check the seasoning, and remove from the heat.

Place the lobsters in a steamer and steam 5 minutes to partially cook them. Cut the lobsters into serving pieces and place in a large sauté pan. Cover with the sauce, adding a little water if the sauce is too thick. Bring to a simmer and cook 15 minutes, covered, basting with the sauce from time to time. When the cooking is finished, set aside, covered.

While the lobsters are cooking, bring a large pot of salted water to a boil for the pasta. Boil the linguine until it is al dente, about 7 minutes, drain, and toss with the remaining oil.

To serve, transfer the lobsters to a platter, leaving about 2 cups of the sauce in the pan. Add the linguine to the pan, toss with the sauce, and serve on the side.

🍷 Brunello di Montalcino, Barolo,
or Fiano di Avellino

POULTRY

CRISPY POUSSINS WITH CHANTERELLES 142

THREE-GLASS CHICKEN 145

POLLO BORRACHO, DRUNKEN CHICKEN 146

CHICKEN POT PIE 148

HONEY-SOY QUAILS WITH FOIE GRAS 150

GRILLED CHICKEN PAILLARD WITH ARUGULA SALAD
AND CRISPY ONIONS 152

POACHED DUCK WITH FARRO 154

CRISP FARMHOUSE DUCK 156

CRISPY POUSSINS WITH CHANTERELLES

FLEUR DE SEL

Cyril Renaud's intimate French restaurant in the Flatiron district does not pretend to be a bistro or brasserie—labels that many places apply to themselves, often incorrectly. Instead it's just a warm, comforting, and unpretentious place that has drawn a steady clientele for Renaud's reliable and appealing French fare. But wait: Chef Renaud is also the owner of another place, Bar Breton, a few blocks north. It is more brash and informal, actually a modest brasserie, with a list of beers and ciders, serving crepes and seafood in the style of Renaud's native Brittany.

4 poussins, split and flattened,
  backbone removed

Salt and freshly ground black pepper

½ cup extra virgin olive or grapeseed oil

1 pound chanterelles, trimmed and
  halved vertically

1 pound baby spinach

2 tablespoons minced fresh
  tarragon leaves

A well-balanced Bordeaux from
St. Julien, displaying both fruit and
terroir character

If fresh chanterelles are not
available, oyster mushrooms cut
in 1-inch pieces or small shiitake
mushroom caps can be substituted.

Preheat the oven to 500 degrees. Rinse and dry the poussins. Season them skin side only with salt and pepper. Heat half the oil in a large skillet until very hot, add 2 poussins, skin side down, and sauté until browned, about 10 minutes. Remove them from the pan and transfer them, skin side up, to a roasting pan or baking dish large enough to hold all 4 poussins in a single layer. Repeat with the remaining oil and poussins. Set the skillet aside.

Roast the birds until they are cooked through, about 25 minutes, basting two or three times with the pan juices. When done, remove the pan from the oven and cover with foil to keep warm. Turn off the oven.

Discard all but 3 tablespoons of the fat in the skillet. Add the chanterelles and sauté over medium heat until they are just tender, about 6 minutes. Season with salt and pepper. Transfer them to an ovenproof dish and place in the turned-off oven. Add the baby spinach to the skillet and sauté until wilted, about 4 minutes. Season with salt and pepper and scatter with tarragon.

Place the spinach on a warm platter. Place the poussins on top of the spinach. Spread the chanterelles around and drizzle with the pan juices from the poussins. Serve.

THREE-GLASS CHICKEN

> *The almost minimalist dining room* only hints at its Chinese connection. But the menu leaves no doubt. Jimmy Chin's Midtown restaurant combines regional Chinese cooking with some inventive specialties such as Grand Marnier Shrimp. Three-Glass Chicken is a homestyle dish, so named because traditionally the chicken pieces are smothered with a glass of soy sauce, a glass of rice wine, and a glass of water, and slowly baked. That does not quite describe the proportions or the quicker, stove-top method, but Chin Chin's is a lusty, well-seasoned version.

SERVES 2

4 Chinese dried black mushrooms
2 whole chicken legs and thighs
3 tablespoons peanut oil
2 tablespoons Asian sesame oil
10 garlic cloves, peeled
12 thin slices fresh ginger
1 small green chile, sliced
2 scallions, trimmed and minced
1 tablespoon minced cilantro leaves
½ cup rice wine or dry sherry
¼ cup soy sauce
1 tablespoon sugar
¼ teaspoon freshly ground white
   pepper
¼ teaspoon freshly ground black
   pepper
Steamed long-grain rice,
   for serving

Place the mushrooms in a bowl and cover with hot water. Set aside to soak.

Separate the chicken legs and thighs at the joint. Use a heavy cleaver to whack them into 1½-inch pieces, right through the bone. You should have 14 to 16 bite-size pieces. Pat them dry with paper towels.

Heat the peanut oil to very hot in a wok or skillet, add the chicken pieces, and cook, turning, to brown on all sides, about 10 minutes. Remove the chicken, draining it well, and discard the oil. Drain the mushrooms and pat them dry. Add the sesame oil to the wok, then the mushrooms, garlic, ginger, chile, scallions, and cilantro. Stir-fry over high heat for 2 minutes. Add the rice wine, soy sauce, and sugar, and stir. Return the chicken to the wok. Bring to a boil, season with the white and black pepper, reduce the heat to a simmer, cover, and cook for 8 minutes. Steamed rice is a must alongside.

> The Chinese do not simply cut up a chicken at the joints, but go on to chop it into small, almost bite-size pieces irrespective of the bird's skeleton. That way everyone gets the same size pieces.

 An Alsatian gewürztraminer

POLLO BORRACHO, DRUNKEN CHICKEN
ZARELA

Women have long been responsible for the strength of the Mexican kitchen, keeping the flame of traditional cooking alive and passing it down through generations. So it comes as no surprise that in New York, where women chefs are in a decided minority, the Mexican women also shine. Zarela Martinez, who was discovered by Craig Claiborne of the *New York Times*, is in the forefront. At her restaurant, Zarela, she produces crowd-pleasing margaritas, guacamole, chilaquiles, enchiladas, and other staples of the cuisine, along with less well-known regional specialties and some inventive dishes, such as this chicken cooked with tequila.

½ cup dry sherry

½ cup golden raisins

½ cup all-purpose flour

Salt and freshly ground white
   pepper

1 frying chicken (about 3½ pounds),
   cut in 8 pieces

½ cup corn oil

1 medium onion, peeled and thinly
   sliced

3 garlic cloves, peeled and sliced

½ cup whole blanched almonds

½ cup small pimento-stuffed olives

2 or more pickled serrano chiles,
   sliced, optional

1 tablespoon cornstarch

1½ cups chicken stock

1 cup silver or reposado tequila

⅓ to ½ cup sherry vinegar

1 tablespoon sugar

> In Mexico this dish would have a more pronounced tartness from as much as a cup of white vinegar. Using sherry vinegar tones it down a bit, but feel free to increase the amount.

Warm the sherry in a small saucepan, add the raisins, and set aside to soak at least 20 minutes. Meanwhile, whisk together the flour and salt and pepper to taste in a shallow dish. Add the chicken pieces and turn to coat them evenly.

Heat the oil in a large skillet to very hot, but not smoking. Add the chicken and sauté until it is golden brown on all sides, about 10 minutes. Transfer it to a 4-quart casserole.

Preheat the oven to 350 degrees.

Discard all but 2 tablespoons of fat from the skillet. Add the onion and garlic and sauté over medium heat, scraping up any browned bits from the pan, until the onion is golden, about 4 minutes. Add the almonds and cook for 2 minutes. Add the olives, the pickled serranos if using, and the raisins with remaining sherry, and cook for 2 minutes more.

In a separate dish, dissolve the cornstarch in about ¼ cup of the chicken stock. Add remaining 1¼ cups of the chicken stock and the tequila to the skillet, and bring to a simmer. Add ⅓ cup of the vinegar and the sugar, and give it a taste. Add additional vinegar as desired to make the sauce pleasingly tart with a touch of sweetness. Stir in the cornstarch mixture, bring to a boil, reduce the heat, and simmer the sauce until it thickens somewhat, about 10 minutes. Pour it over the chicken in the casserole, cover, and bake about 20 minutes, until the chicken is done. Adjust the seasonings, adding more salt, pepper, or vinegar, as desired, and serve.

 A full-bodied viognier

CHICKEN POT PIE

Is it a restaurant or a club? When Graydon Carter, the editor of Vanity Fair, took over this venerable tourist magnet in Greenwich Village, he reopened it without publishing a phone number. Yet people flock to The Waverly Inn nightly to mingle with the boldface names and the less-notable, all eating and drinking well. The restaurant has been restored, and its mantra is now comfort food, but elevated to a higher plane. Macaroni and cheese is infused with truffle oil, for example, and the humble chicken pot pie benefits from a lid of French puff pastry. The preparation is time-consuming, but much of the work can be done in advance and the end result is well worth the effort—this may be the best pot pie on the planet.

SERVES 4

2 large chicken breast halves, with skin and bone, 12 to 16 ounces each

3 chicken thighs, with skin and bone

3 chicken legs, with skin and bone

1 medium onion, quartered

2 stalks celery, cut into 3-inch pieces

2 large carrots, peeled and cut in half crosswise

Salt and freshly ground black pepper

Place the chicken parts, onion, celery and carrots in a large pot, cover with water, season with salt and pepper, and bring to a simmer. Cook, skimming the surface occasionally, until the chicken is done, about 25 minutes. Remove the chicken to a bowl.

Strain the broth from the chicken into a saucepan. Reserve the celery and carrots in a dish. Boil the broth until it is reduced to 1½ cups. Season with salt and pepper.

Melt 3 tablespoons of the butter in a small saucepan. Whisk in the flour and cook until well blended. Gradually add the broth, whisking constantly until the sauce is thick and smooth. Whisk in the cream, Worcestershire, Tabasco, and salt and pepper to taste.

4 tablespoons (½ stick) unsalted butter

3 tablespoons all-purpose flour

2 tablespoons heavy cream

1 teaspoon Worcestershire sauce

½ teaspoon Tabasco, or to taste

3 ounces medium-size cremini mushrooms, quartered

8 small pearl onions, blanched and peeled

1 cup frozen garden peas

1 pound frozen puff pastry, preferably made with butter, thawed

1 large egg, lightly beaten

This recipe is a production, but the good news is that it can be assembled in advance and refrigerated until two hours before serving. Remove it from the refrigerator and allow it to come to room temperature before baking it.

The pot pie can also be divided into individual 2-cup casseroles, each with its own puff pastry top. That way, the recipe will provide about 6 servings.

Heat the remaining butter in a medium skillet. Add the mushrooms and sauté until just tender. Place in a large bowl. Slice the carrots 1 inch thick at an angle and add. Slice the celery ½ inch thick and add. Fold in the pearl onions and peas. Remove the skin and bones from the chicken and cut or tear the meat into large bite-size pieces. Fold in with the vegetables. Fold in the sauce. Transfer this mixture to a 2½- to 3-quart baking dish that is at least 2 inches deep.

Preheat the oven to 450 degrees. Cut the puff pastry to fit the dish, allowing an inch of overhang all around. Crimp the edges to the rim of the dish. Brush with beaten egg and cut a hole in the center to allow steam to escape. Bake until the crust has browned and the filling is bubbling, about 25 minutes. Serve.

You need a wine that is round, buttery and soft, like a toasty, creamy Meursault Villages.

HONEY-SOY QUAILS WITH FOIE GRAS

New York is a tough market, as Gordon Ramsay, the Michelin three-star English celebrity chef found out. When he opened his eponymous restaurant, with the attached café, Maze, in the London New York hotel, Ramsay was not welcomed with open arms. He had to fight to prove his merit, and he has done so successfully, in both restaurants. His food is more French than English, as this quail dish made with foie gras clearly demonstrates.

¼ cup extra virgin olive oil

6 shallots, sliced

8 fresh thyme sprigs

2 bay leaves

3 garlic cloves, thinly sliced

1 cup dry white wine

1 cup Madeira

2 cups chicken stock, approximately

2 tablespoons soy sauce

3 tablespoons lavender or acacia
  honey

4 quails, breasts deboned,
  butterflied

4 slices fresh duck foie gras, each
  about 1-ounce

Sea salt and freshly ground black
  pepper

½ cup fig or apple chutney, optional

Vacuum-sealed individual slices of fresh duck foie gras are now sold in fancy food shops.

It is important to work quickly when cooking the foie gras so the outside sears but the interior remains medium-rare.

The chutney can be homemade or store-bought, but it should not be Indian-style Major Grey mango chutney.

This dish can also be served for four, as a first course.

Heat 1 tablespoon of the olive oil in a small skillet, add the shallots, and cook until they become translucent, about 7 minutes. Add the thyme, bay leaves, and garlic. Sauté briefly, then add the white wine. Cook, stirring, until the wine is reduced by half. Add the Madeira and 1 cup of the chicken stock and cook until reduced by half again; stir in the soy sauce and honey. Simmer until the sauce has thickened somewhat and is reduced to barely 1 cup of glaze. Strain into a bowl and cover to keep warm.

Dry the quails. In a skillet large enough to hold them, heat the remaining olive oil and sear the quails, skin side down, over medium-high heat until golden, about 10 minutes. Discard all but 2 tablespoons fat from the skillet. Lower the heat, add half of the remaining chicken stock and cook gently until the quails are done, a few minutes more, using more stock as needed to keep them moist. Remove from the heat and tent with foil to keep warm.

Just before serving, heat a medium-size cast-iron skillet until very hot. Season the slices of foie gras with salt and pepper, place them in the skillet, and cook over medium-high heat for less than a minute on each side. The slices should be medium-rare. Do not overcook.

Place the quails in the center of each of 2 dinner plates. Top each with a slice of foie gras and drizzle the sauce over both. Serve immediately with chutney on the side.

Shawn Paul, the sommelier, suggests a kabinett riesling from the Mosel.

GRILLED CHICKEN PAILLARD WITH ARUGULA SALAD AND CRISPY ONIONS

HARRY'S CAFÉ

> *Harry Poulokakos himself* is almost as much a landmark as India House, the building dominating Hanover Square where his steak house and café are located. His restaurants attract the money managers, brokers, and bank presidents who work and often, in recent years, live in the downtown area. They come to unwind at lunch and after office hours, for a drink, a hamburger, a steak, and perhaps a first-rate bottle of wine. The cellars at Harry's restaurants are among the deepest and most quality-driven in the city.

SERVES 4

½ tablespoon Dijon mustard

3 tablespoons red wine vinegar

½ cup olive oil

Salt and freshly ground pepper

4 skinless, boneless chicken breast halves, about 1¾ pounds total

Canola oil for deep-frying

1 cup flour

2 medium-large onions, sliced thin and separated into rings

1 bunch arugula, rinsed, dried, heavy stems removed

1 cup crumbled blue cheese

Whisk together the mustard, vinegar, 5 tablespoons of the olive oil, and salt and pepper. Reserve.

Butterfly the chicken breasts, place each in a plastic bag, and pound thin. Brush with the remaining olive oil and season with salt and pepper. Set aside.

Preheat a grill if using. Preheat the oven to 200 degrees. Line a baking sheet with parchment.

Heat the canola oil in a large, deep saucepan. Have several thicknesses of paper towel ready. Place the flour in a resealable plastic bag and toss in some of the onion rings. Make sure they are well coated, then shake off any excess flour. Fry the onions, in batches if necessary, for a few minutes over medium-high heat until golden brown, turning them once. Drain the onions on the paper towel, sprinkle with salt and pepper, and transfer them to the baking sheet as they are done and keep them warm in the oven.

Toss the arugula and blue cheese together in a bowl. Give the vinaigrette a quick whisking, then pour it over the salad and toss again.

This is a fabulous dish to serve in warm weather, when it's fun to light the grill. It can also be made with veal scaloppini.

Most recipes recommend pounding chicken or veal between sheets of waxed paper or parchment paper. Plastic bags work extremely well, too.

If you are not using a grill, preheat a grill pan. Sear the chicken on the grill or in the pan until lightly browned and cooked through, 2 to 3 minutes on each side. Place the chicken on a platter or on individual dinner plates. Top the chicken with the arugula salad and then the onions. Serve.

Ivan Mitankin, the wine director, would opt for a dry riesling from the Mosel-Saar-Ruwer region of Germany for a white, or a Burgundy, an Haut Côte de Nuits, for a red.

POACHED DUCK WITH FARRO

A small and unassuming restaurant a few steps below street level does not sound like a recipe for success, especially in Greenwich Village. But Blue Hill, a half-block from Washington Square, has made its mark precisely because it offers elegant food in a subdued, informal setting. Dan Barber, who started as a caterer, has developed a loyal clientele, both here and at Stone Barns, his restaurant on a Rockefeller estate in Tarrytown, New York. For this gently cooked duck breast he discards the fat and skin. But do not be fooled. He substitutes butter to insulate the tender meat.

SERVES 6 TO 8

Salt

2 cups farro (Italian spelt grain, similar to bulgur wheat)

2 cups tiny pearl onions

½ pound (2 sticks) plus 1 tablespoon unsalted butter

½ cup chicken stock

1 teaspoon sugar

Freshly ground black pepper

4 *magret* (moulard duck breasts)

1 cup dry white wine

1 fresh thyme sprig

1 shallot, peeled and thinly sliced

1¼ cups heavy cream

2 cups veal stock

2 cups dry red wine

1 tablespoon Dijon mustard

Fleur de sel, for garnish

Bring 2 quarts of salted water to a boil. Add the farro and cook until just tender, about 25 minutes. Drain thoroughly and place in a large skillet.

While the farro is cooking, place the onions in a bowl, cover with hot water, and set aside for 10 minutes. Peel the onions, trim, and place in a sauté pan with 1 tablespoon of the butter, the chicken stock, sugar, and salt and pepper to taste. Place a piece of parchment paper directly on the onions, and simmer until the onions are tender and the liquid is syrupy, about 10 minutes. Add the onions to the farro and set aside covered, ready to reheat just before serving.

Use a small knife to separate the skin and fat from the duck breasts. The skin and fat should come off quite easily; you will not be using them for this recipe but for more on them, see the tip, opposite. Season the duck breasts with salt and pepper.

Combine the white wine, thyme, and shallot in a 3-quart saucepan large enough to hold 2 of the duck breasts in one layer. Cook the wine mixture over medium-high heat until

You can place the slabs of skin and fat in a single layer in a baking dish. Place in a 200-degree oven for about an hour, until the fat has been rendered out and the skin has started to brown. Now you can toss out the skin. Strain the fat into a jar and reserve it in the refrigerator. You'll have about 2 cups of fresh duck fat to use for sautéing. Use it for the Goose Fat Potatoes, page 194.

it barely films the bottom of the pan. Add the cream and reduce the mixture to ⅔ cup. Strain and return the cream to the saucepan; place over very low heat. Add the remaining ½ pound of butter, ½ tablespoon at a time, whisking it in after each addition. Do not allow the sauce to boil. When all the butter has been incorporated, place 2 of the duck breasts in the saucepan. The sauce should just about cover them. Cook at a bare simmer, swirling the pan to keep the sauce moving, for 4 minutes. Turn the duck breasts in the sauce and cook for 4 more minutes. Remove the duck breasts, scraping as much sauce as possible from them back into the saucepan. Place the cooked duck breasts on a platter and cover with foil. Repeat with the remaining 2 duck breasts. When they have cooked for their 8 minutes, transfer them to the platter and cover with foil. Set aside at least 20 minutes. Discard the butter sauce.

While the duck is resting, in a small saucepan boil down the veal stock until it is reduced to ¾ cup. Boil down the red wine in a separate saucepan until you have just ¾ cup. Combine the veal stock and red wine reductions, whisk in the mustard, and season to taste with salt and pepper.

Reheat the farro mixture and place portions on your dinner plates. Slice the duck breasts on an angle and arrange slices on top of the farro. Garnish with a little *fleur de sel*. Reheat the red wine sauce and spoon it around the plates. Serve immediately.

A medium- to full-bodied pinot noir from Oregon or coastal or central California, or a Burgundy

CRISP FARMHOUSE DUCK

THE FOUR SEASONS

The incomparable four seasons, designed by Philip Johnson for the Mies van der Rohe Seagram Building, is a landmark that attracts powerful names to lunch in the Grill Room, and those who wish to dine well on innovative American cuisine to the Pool Room. The seasonal theme that set the restaurant apart when it first opened in 1959 continues. The flowers change. The food is seasonal, too, relying on timely ingredients, a concept that was devised by the late Joseph Baum, the driving force behind a number of the city's most stunning restaurants. Today it's the way all fine restaurants operate. But one main dish ignores the seasons. The gorgeously lacquered roast duck, brought to the dining room and carved tableside, is as much a signature of The Four Seasons as the perennial chocolate velvet cake.

SERVES 2 TO 4

1 (5- to 6-pound) fresh duck

1 (1-inch) piece fresh ginger, peeled and sliced thin

Grated zest of ½ orange

2 garlic cloves, peeled and crushed

2 tablespoons honey

½ cup soy sauce

1½ teaspoons black peppercorns, crushed

1½ tablespoons bitter orange marmalade

⅓ cup fresh orange juice

1 tablespoon Grand Marnier

1 tablespoon red wine vinegar

1 tablespoon tomato paste

⅓ cup dry red wine

½ cup duck or chicken stock

Salt and freshly ground black pepper

Segments from 1 orange

Rinse the duck, pull out all the excess fat, remove the giblets, and cut off the wingtips and the excess skin at the neck. Save the wingtips and giblets for stock, if you wish. Using a sharp paring knife, make lots of ¼-inch incisions along the back of the duck. They'll allow the fat to drain out during cooking.

Place the duck on a wire rack set on a rimmed baking sheet and refrigerate it uncovered for 48 hours. The idea is to dry out the duck so the skin will crisp up better.

Combine the ginger, orange zest, garlic, honey, soy sauce, and peppercorns in a bowl. Cover and leave at room temperature overnight. Strain this marinade and discard the solids.

Remove the duck from the refrigerator and brush it all over with half the marinade. Leave it for 20 minutes, then brush it with all but 2 tablespoons of the marinade. Refrigerate the unused marinade.

Refrigerate the duck again, for 24 hours more.

You may choose, of course, not to bother with the sauce, and just serve the duck au naturel.

Accomplishing this extra-crisp duck is a four-day project, so plan accordingly. At the Four Seasons the duck is actually dried in the Chinese manner, by hanging it to allow the air to circulate. But putting it on a rack in the refrigerator, uncovered, is an acceptable compromise.

Raphael First Label Merlot 1999 or an American merlot, preferably from Long Island

Remove the duck from the refrigerator 5 hours before serving time. Make sure one oven rack is completely clean, because the duck is going to sit directly on it.

About 2½ hours before serving, preheat the oven to 375 degrees. Place a roasting pan with ¼ inch of water in it on the lowest rack in the oven. Position the clean rack in the middle of the oven. Place the duck, breast side up, on the middle rack, directly over the pan of water. The roasting time is 1½ to 2 hours, depending on the size of the duck, at the end of which your duck should be a gorgeous, shiny mahogany color, and slightly puffed. When it's done, transfer it to a cutting board and allow it to rest for 20 minutes.

To make the sauce, mix the marmalade, orange juice, Grand Marnier, vinegar, tomato paste, wine, and stock in a saucepan. Add the reserved marinade and simmer it for about 10 minutes. Strain it, add salt and pepper to taste and the orange segments, and keep it warm until you carve the duck. Spoon the sauce over the duck portions.

MEAT

LAMB TAGINE WITH ISRAELI COUSCOUS
MARSEILLE

Marseille, the city, is the melting pot of France, and also a gateway
to North Africa. Thus it should come as no surprise that the chef at Marseille,
Alex Urena, offers a *tagine* here to represent the restaurant. A *tagine* is both a
type of braised dish and also the vessel in which it is cooked: a rimmed, shallow,
glazed terra-cotta platter with a distinctive conical lid. Typically, the inside of
the lid is left unglazed so that the steam that rises as the food is cooked can
actually be absorbed into the clay and not condense back on the food. The
result is a more concentrated sauce. At Marseille, Urena serves a cuisine that
represents many areas of the Mediterranean, all in a vaguely Art Deco brasserie
setting. The owner, Simon Oren, has a love affair with France, as represented
by some of his other restaurants, including Nice Matin and Pigalle.

2 pounds boneless leg of lamb,
  in 2-inch cubes

Salt and freshly ground black pepper

1 tablespoon ground cardamom

1 tablespoon ground cumin

6 tablespoons extra virgin olive oil

1 medium parsnip, peeled and diced

2 carrots, peeled and diced

2 medium onions, peeled and
  finely diced

¼ cup tomato paste

1 cup dry red wine

¼ cup Madeira

1 cup veal stock

1 tablespoon lemon juice

1 bay leaf

1 rosemary sprig

5 fresh thyme sprigs

1 cup Israeli couscous (very large
  grain couscous)

2 cups hot chicken stock

1 tablespoon minced mint leaves

Like most stewed or braised dishes, this *tagine* benefits from resting, then reheating.

Although the couscous can simply be reheated in its saucepan, if it is made well in advance, it can be spread out on a shallow baking pan, coated lightly with olive oil, and set aside. It should then be reheated with some additional stock.

Season the meat with salt, pepper, and ½ tablespoon each of the cardamom and cumin. Use your hands to massage the seasonings into the meat.

In a large, heavy sauté pan heat 2 tablespoons of the oil. Add the lamb and, without crowding it, sear it over high heat until browned on all sides. You may have to sear it in batches. Remove the meat from the pan and add the parsnip, carrots, and half of the onions. Sauté them over low heat—the term the chefs use for this is to "sweat" them—until they're tender but not browned. Add the remaining ½ tablespoon each of the cardamom and cumin, stir, and then stir in the tomato paste. Add the red wine and Madeira and increase the heat so the wine can reduce by half.

If you own a bona fide terra-cotta *tagine* that is at least 12 inches in diameter (to fit all the ingredients), transfer the cooked vegetables and wine to it. Add the seared meat and any juices, and the veal stock, lemon juice, bay leaf, rosemary, and 4 sprigs of the thyme. Cover your *tagine* and either place it on very low heat on the top of your stove, where you will let the contents barely simmer for 2 hours, or put it in a 300-degree oven. Without a *tagine*, use a nice casserole in a 300-degree oven.

After 2 hours, remove the *tagine* from the heat and set the dish aside for at least an hour. Reheat it for a few minutes when you're ready to serve.

For the couscous heat the remaining 4 tablespoons of the oil in a heavy saucepan. Add the remaining onions and sauté them until they're tender. Stir in the couscous, then add the chicken stock, salt and pepper to taste, and the last sprig of thyme. Cover and cook until the couscous is tender and all the stock is absorbed, about 20 minutes. Fold in the mint. Serve with the *tagine*.

 A red Rioja would complement the dish.

LAMB SHANKS WITH CHILES IN PARCHMENT

ROSA MEXICANO

Josefina Howard, the now-legendary force behind Rosa Mexicano, was among the first in New York to create a Mexican destination for fine dining. Her restaurant near Sutton Place always honored authentic Mexican ingredients, and is filled with Mexican crafts. She was also the originator of the much-copied concept of making guacamole fresh at tableside. Now there is a branch of Rosa Mexicano near Lincoln Center and another near Union Square. The food at all restaurants is much the same.

SERVES 4

8 dried *pasilla* chiles, cut open, seeds and veins removed

8 dried *guajillo* chiles, cut open, seeds and veins removed

4 lamb shanks, about 14 ounces each

¼ cup white vinegar

¼ cup dark Mexican beer

1 tablespoon silver tequila

¼ teaspoon cumin seeds

5 whole cloves

½ teaspoon dried oregano, preferably Mexican

4 garlic cloves

Salt

8 fresh or dried avocado leaves, optional

Lime wedges and warm yellow corn tortillas for serving

Toast the *pasilla* and *guajillo* chiles in a toaster oven or in a dry skillet about 3 minutes until the insides turn light brown. Place in a bowl, cover with warm water, and soak for 15 minutes.

Scrape away enough meat from the bottom of the lamb shanks to expose about 1½ inches of bone.

Preheat the oven to 300 degrees.

Drain the chiles and place in a blender with the vinegar, beer, tequila, cumin, cloves, oregano, and garlic. Add enough water to make a thick, textured puree. Season to taste with salt.

Place each lamb shank on a large piece of parchment paper. Spoon some of the sauce onto each lamb shank and rub into the meat, taking care not to spread it on the bone. Top each lamb shank with 2 avocado leaves, if using.

Wrap the shanks in the parchment and tie around the bone with butcher's string. Place shanks on a foil-lined baking pan, place in the oven, and bake about 2½ hours, until tender when pierced with the point of a knife (open the parchment to test).

Place each lamb shank, still wrapped, on a plate. Serve and open the parchment at the dinner table. Pass the lime and tortillas at the table.

Cabernet sauvignon-merlot blend from Mexico. A cabernet sauvignon from Chile would be another good option.

RACK OF LAMB WITH WHITE BEANS

LE PÉRIGORD

In some respects, Le Périgord is a neighborhood restaurant. It serves the residents of Sutton Place high-rises as well as diplomats from the United Nations nearby. Georges Briguet, the owner, has continental grace, pampering his elite clientele and seeing to it that their appetites are tempted by French food that is never out of bounds. The room is comfortable and has a pretty glow about it. Fresh flowers, fine tableware, and waiters with great poise round out the picture. A very basic rack of lamb comes on a bed of white beans brought into focus with the peppery sharpness of celery root and the addition of seasonal fresh peas.

6 ounces dried French coco beans (large white beans) or cannellini beans

1 small celery root, about ¾ pound, peeled and quartered

2 carrots, peeled and quartered

1 bouquet garni (see tips)

Salt and freshly ground black pepper

2 racks of lamb, Frenched (see tips)

1 pound fresh peas, shelled

2 tablespoons unsalted butter

Coco beans are dried large white beans, but cannellini beans are a good substitute.

A bouquet garni is a couple of bay leaves, a sprig of thyme, and a few sprigs of flat-leaf parsley tied together or wrapped in a piece of cheesecloth so they can be removed easily.

A Frenched rack of lamb is one that has the meat scraped off the ends of the bones to make for a neater presentation. Little ruffled paper caps are sometimes put on the bones for serving.

Place the beans in a bowl, cover with water to a depth of 2 inches, and soak overnight. Drain the beans, transfer them to a large saucepan, and add the celery root, carrots, and bouquet garni. Add water to cover all the ingredients to a depth of 2 inches. Bring to a boil and simmer until the beans are tender, about 40 minutes. Drain them.

Remove and discard the carrot pieces and the bouquet garni. Cut the celery root in ½-inch dice, fold it into the beans, and place in a clean saucepan. Season to taste with salt and pepper.

Preheat the oven to 425 degrees. Season the lamb with salt and pepper and place in a roasting pan, fat side up. Roast 20 to 25 minutes, until an instant-read thermometer registers 125 degrees when inserted into the meat. Remove the lamb from the oven and set aside 10 minutes.

Bring a small pot of salted water to a boil, add the peas, cook 3 minutes, drain, and place briefly in a bowl of ice water to set the color. Drain the cooled peas well and fold into the bean mixture. Add the butter and reheat the beans, celery root, and peas.

To serve, carve the racks into chops. Spoon a large mound of the beans onto each of 4 warmed plates, arrange the lamb on the beans, and serve immediately.

 A St. Émilion

ROASTED BABY GOAT WITH FINGERLINGS AND SHALLOTS

SCARPETTA

Ever since he started at L'Impero—now Convivio with a new chef (see page 78)—Scott Conant's signature dish has been this lush and tender braised goat. When he opened Scarpetta, he took it with him. The restaurant's name means "little shoe" and refers to the piece of bread that a satisfied diner uses to mop up the sauce left on a plate. This dish certainly qualifies for that treatment.

SERVES 6

3½ pounds boneless goat meat, the younger the better, in 1½-inch cubes

¾ cup extra virgin olive oil

9 fresh rosemary sprigs

6 large garlic cloves, crushed

Pinch crushed red chili flakes

Kosher salt and freshly ground black pepper

4 cups chicken stock

1½ pounds fingerling potatoes, peeled and quartered lengthwise

1 very large shallot, peeled and sliced lengthwise

1 tablespoon minced flat-leaf parsley leaves

Trim any excess fat from the goat. Place it in a large bowl with ½ cup of the olive oil, 3 sprigs of the rosemary, the garlic, crushed chili, 1 teaspoon salt, and 1 teaspoon pepper. Rub the meat all over with these ingredients, cover the bowl, and refrigerate the meat overnight. The next day remove the meat, reserving the garlic and rosemary.

Heat a tablespoon of the oil in a heavy, 4- to 6-quart casserole. Sear the meat in shifts, without crowding it in the pan, until it is lightly browned on all sides. Remove it to a bowl as it is done. When the meat has been seared, add about half of the stock to the casserole, scraping the bottom.

Preheat the oven to 300 degrees. Return the meat and the marinade ingredients to the casserole, along with any accumulated meat juices, bring to a simmer, cover, and place in the oven until the meat is fork-tender, about 2½ hours, adding the additional stock during the cooking.

Use a slotted spoon to transfer the meat to a bowl. Cover the bowl and set it aside at room temperature for an hour or so, or refrigerate it for a longer period, even overnight. Strain the liquid in the casserole into a separate bowl. Refrigerate an hour or longer. Skim off the fat.

Farmers' markets are good places to find goat meat, as are specialty butchers. There are also online sources. Try to buy the boneless kind because it will be much easier to handle and to eat.

A full-bodied, spicy red gaglioppo from Apulia, in the heel of Italy, would be our choice for a wine to pour with this rustic dish.

Place the potatoes in a saucepan with salted water to cover and par-cook for 6 minutes. Drain. Heat the remaining oil in a large skillet, add the potatoes, and sauté them over medium heat until they are barely beginning to brown. Add the shallot and continue to cook until the potatoes and shallot are golden. Season with salt and pepper. Set aside off the heat. Scatter the parsley on top.

Return the sauce to the casserole and boil it until it has reduced and thickened a bit. Season with salt and pepper. Return the goat to the casserole and reheat it, basting it with the sauce.

To serve, spoon the goat and the sauce into a rimmed platter. Surround it with the potatoes and shallots if there is room, or serve these in a separate dish.

RACK OF PORK WITH MUSTARD-MOLASSES GLAZE AND SOUR MASH SAUCE

BAR AMERICAIN

Chef Bobby Flay's latest contribution to the New York scene is in one of the three brash, spacious locations that have anchored the Equitable Building since 1986. Bar Americain is an American brasserie serving Chef Flay's typically lusty food, which is often bolstered with a taste of the South. His technique of brining pork before roasting it adds flavor and juiciness that is often absent from today's extra-lean meat.

SERVES 4 TO 6

4 cups apple juice

Kosher salt

¾ cup light brown sugar

1 medium onion, peeled and
quartered

10 black peppercorns

½ teaspoon yellow mustard seeds

8 fresh thyme sprigs

2 bay leaves

4-pound center-cut rack of pork,
excess fat trimmed

Freshly ground black pepper

2 tablespoons extra virgin olive oil

¼ cup Dijon mustard

2 tablespoons whole grain mustard

2 tablespoons molasses

3 shallots, peeled and diced

2 cups Jack Daniels whiskey

2 cups chicken stock

2 tablespoons cold unsalted butter,
in small pieces

Bring the apple juice, ½ cup salt, ½ cup of the sugar and the onion, peppercorns, mustard seeds, thyme, bay leaves, and 2 cups water to a simmer in a 4-quart pot. Cook, stirring, until the sugar and salt have dissolved, about 10 minutes. Let this brine cool completely. Place the pork in a large, heavy-duty plastic bag with a zipper closure. Pour in the brine, seal, place in a bowl and refrigerate overnight.

The next day, remove the pork from the brine, pat it dry with paper towels, and season with salt and pepper.

Preheat the oven to 425 degrees. Heat the oil over high heat in a skillet large enough to hold the pork and brown it on all sides until golden brown, 8 to 10 minutes. Do not clean the skillet.

In a small bowl, whisk together the mustards, molasses, and salt and pepper to taste. Reserve.

Transfer the pork to a baking pan and roast it, fat side up, for 25 to 30 minutes or until an instant-read thermometer registers 150 degrees when inserted in the thickest part of the meat. Brush the molasses mixture over the pork several times during the last 10 minutes of cooking. Remove the pork from the oven and set it aside on a carving board.

2 tablespoons finely chopped
   flat-leaf parsley leaves
1 cup apple butter, homemade
   or store-bought

Adding butter as you finish a
sauce gives it great body and
sheen, especially if you use a high-
fat, European-style butter. Be sure
the heat is very low, or the sauce
will not hold together.

Roasting the pork to 150 degrees,
then letting it rest, brings the
internal temperature to 155 degrees
or so, enough to keep it tinged with
pink in the center and juicy, but also
safely cooked through.

Heat the skillet with its remaining fat and cook the shallots
over medium heat until soft, about 5 minutes. Add the Jack
Daniels and cook until almost completely reduced. Add
the chicken stock and the remaining brown sugar and
cook, reducing until the sauce coats the back of a wooden
spoon, about 10 minutes. Set aside off the heat.

Cut the pork into individual chops. Return the sauce to
low heat and whisk in the butter bit by bit, season with salt
and pepper and stir in the parsley.

Serve each chop with a spoonful or two of sauce drizzled
over it and a dollop of apple butter alongside.

An off-dry Riesling, like a spätlese would be the
white wine of choice, and for a red, an earthy
Oregon pinot noir or a racy syrah from the Rhone.

SAUTÉED VEAL MEDALLIONS WITH THYME

AUREOLE

Charles Palmer, the chef and owner of Aureole, describes himself as "a big American guy," and knows that his food reflects his personality. It's robust, abundant. But at the same time, it has the kind of elegance that befits its setting in a lovely Upper East Side brownstone. For 20 years, the restaurant was a special-occasion magnet for New Yorkers and visitors whose main objective is fine food in a gracious setting. It has now moved to midtown, near Bryant Park. Palmer's interpretation of American food comes richly accented with French, Italian, Middle Eastern, and Asian influences. His generosity of spirit goes beyond the walls of the restaurant. He encourages chefs who work with him, and spends time as a mentor to high school students in the city.

SERVES 6

3 tablespoons extra virgin olive oil

4 shallots, peeled and diced

3 tablespoons minced garlic

4 fresh thyme sprigs

2 cups dry white wine

6 cups veal stock (see tip)

Coarse salt and freshly ground black pepper

12 baby carrots, peeled, 1 inch of green top left on

2 teaspoons unsalted butter

12 (3-ounce) veal medallions, ½-inch thick

2 tablespoons minced flat-leaf parsley leaves

Heat 1 tablespoon of the oil in a large saucepan over medium heat. Add the shallots, garlic, and thyme and sauté about 4 minutes, until the shallots have softened. Add the wine and simmer 30 minutes or longer, until the liquid just films the bottom of the pan. Add the stock and simmer, stirring from time to time, about 45 minutes, until reduced to 2 cups. Strain through a fine-mesh sieve into a small saucepan. Season to taste with salt and pepper. Set aside.

Bring a small pot of salted water to a boil. Add the carrots and blanch 3 minutes, until crisp-tender. Drain, refresh under cold water, and pat dry. Melt the butter in a small sauté pan, add the carrots, and sauté a few minutes until heated through. Season to taste with salt and pepper and set aside.

Heat the remaining 2 tablespoons of olive oil in a large sauté pan over medium-high heat. When hot, add half the medallions. Sauté 2 minutes on each side, until lightly browned but still pink in the middle. Remove the meat from the pan, and repeat with the remaining veal.

Place 2 medallions on each of 6 warm dinner plates. Reheat carrots, adding parsley. Place 2 carrots on each plate. Reheat the wine sauce and spoon over the veal. Serve immediately.

Veal is a red wine meat. This dish is especially suited to a pinot noir from Oregon.

Preparing the sauce is time-consuming but it can be done well in advance, even frozen, making the final cooking quick and convenient.

Though restaurants have veal stock on hand, home cooks may not. Fortunately there are excellent ones sold in fine food shops. Look for one that has no starches, gums, or other additives.

WIENER SCHNITZEL

WALLSÉ

> *In a city short on Austrian and German restaurants,* Kurt Gutenbrunner's Wallsé on the edge of Greenwich Village stands out. Its two rooms are almost stark, done in a black and white Josef Hoffmann esthetic. And the cooking decidedly puts to rest any notion that Germanic food is heavy. While remaining loyal to the cuisine of his native Austria, Gutenbrunner takes liberties that give everything an uncommon freshness. Of course, when it comes to dessert, there's richness to spare. The food of Wallsé is also served for breakfast, lunch, midafternoon tea, and dinner uptown, at Café Sabarsky in the Neue Galerie on Fifth Avenue.

SERVES 4

1 pound veal top round cut into 4-ounce scaloppine but not pounded

Salt and freshly ground white pepper

1 cup flour

2 eggs

2 tablespoons heavy cream

2 cups unseasoned bread crumbs, preferably from a bakery

2 cups vegetable oil

½ cup packed flat-leaf parsley leaves, rinsed, well-dried, and coarsely chopped

3 tablespoons unsalted butter

4 lemon wedges

Cucumber or Bibb lettuce salad with vinaigrette dressing, for serving

🍷 An Austrian white wine from the Wachau Valley, especially grüner veltliner or riesling

Place one of the scaloppine in a heavy 1-quart plastic bag and pound it thin with a meat pounder. Repeat with the remaining scaloppine. Place your thin scaloppine on a large platter and season them lightly with salt and pepper.

Place the flour in a shallow bowl large enough to hold one of the scaloppine flat. Place the eggs and cream in a similar bowl, and beat them lightly to blend. Place the bread crumbs in a third similar bowl. Line up the bowls near your stove. Preheat the oven to 175 degrees. Line a baking sheet with parchment. Place a platter covered with several thicknesses of paper towel near the stove. Place a small plate, also covered with paper towel, near the stove.

Heat the oil in an 11- to 12-inch skillet or sauté pan, the deeper the better. If you have a chicken fryer, use it. When the oil is quite hot, place the parsley leaves in a metal mesh strainer, place in the oil, and fry 10 seconds. Remove the parsley, draining it well, and put it on the small plate. Add the butter to the skillet and reduce the heat to medium.

Place a slice of the veal in the flour, coat it well on both sides, and shake off the excess. Place it in the egg, turning to coat both sides, then place it in the bread crumbs,

The most efficient way to handle the coating and cooking is to use one hand for dipping the veal and the other for moving the skillet, so your fingers covered with egg and crumbs do not have to touch the pan.

Keeping the skillet with oil moving results in a lighter breading, one that bubbles up and almost floats on the surface of the veal, which is how a proper wiener schnitzel should be.

coating it well. Shake off any excess. Place it in the skillet and fry it about 1 minute, gently moving the pan in a circular motion so the oil is frothy. When the breading looks bubbly and starts to brown, turn the veal with a fork or tongs. Cook about another minute, then transfer to the paper-lined platter to drain. Repeat with the remaining veal, adjusting your heat so the crumb coating cooks gradually and evenly.

Transfer each of the finished, drained schnitzels to the baking sheet and hold them in the oven until serving time, no more than 15 minutes. Arrange the veal on a platter or on individual plates and garnish with lemon wedges and the fried parsley. Serve with salad.

VEAL PICCATA

ANGELINA'S

> *A restaurant with its soul still bonded to Italy,* Angelina's combines warmth of family with the modern sophistication that fine dining requires today. It has a lovely garden look, and, when the weather permits, outdoor tables under Italian market umbrellas. The kitchen's focus is on upscale Italian food, the kind of menu that everyone has understood as Northern Italian for many years. To its credit, the simple classic Veal Piccata is called just that, and not given the popular but meaningless name of "Veal Francese." The wine cellar offers a well-rounded list of bottles from many regions of Italy as well as selections from France and California.

SERVES 4

1¼ pounds veal for scaloppine,
   pounded thin, in 8 pieces
Salt and freshly ground black pepper
½ cup flour
3 tablespoons extra virgin olive oil
3 tablespoons soft unsalted butter
1 cup dry white wine
½ cup chicken stock
Juice of ½ lemon
1 tablespoon coarsely chopped
   flat-leaf parsley leaves

Dry the veal well, season it with salt and pepper, and dip in flour, shaking off excess.

Heat the oil in a large sauté pan. Sauté the veal about 1 minute on each side, until lightly browned. Transfer to a warm platter. You may have to cook the veal in batches. Add 1 tablespoon of the butter and the wine to the pan. Cook down until the wine films the pan. Lower the heat and add chicken stock, salt and pepper to taste, and the lemon juice. Cook briefly over high heat, then lower the heat and add remaining butter, bit by bit, whisking to combine and emulsify. Return the veal to the pan, and briefly baste with sauce. Transfer the veal to a platter, spoon the sauce over it, sprinkle with parsley, and serve.

 California chardonnay from Napa Valley

> Drying the veal scaloppine will permit it to brown better and faster.

DELMONICO STEAK

The name that Henry Meer selected for his restaurant, City Hall, could not be more appropriate. It's a few blocks from the actual City Hall and from the nearby complex of courthouses and municipal buildings. And it has become a clubhouse of sorts for city officials, lawyers, and judges. The restaurant, a comfortable banquette-filled room in an old cast-iron building, plays on the theme of old New York with historic photographs and a menu that reflects some of the city's venerable dining traditions. The Delmonico Steak, a rib-eye named after a famous nineteenth-century restaurant, is a good example. Meer's version is topped with blue cheese butter. In keeping with his approach to cooking—very contemporary with an emphasis on market-fresh American ingredients—he uses Maytag blue cheese. He is so committed to seasonal freshness in this restaurant that in summer he runs a small farmer's market outside City Hall, where he sells produce from his cousin's farm in Bridgehampton, New York.

SERVES 2

4 ounces (about 1 cup) crumbled domestic blue cheese, preferably Maytag blue

4 tablespoons (½ stick) softened unsalted butter

A few dashes Tabasco

2 rib-eye steaks, preferably dry-aged prime, each about 14 ounces, with bone

Sea salt and freshly ground white pepper

> Allowing the steak to rest after it comes off the fire will guarantee its juiciness. It's also a necessary step to make sure that returning it to the broiler to melt the cheese will not overcook it.

The blue cheese butter that tops the steak can be made well in advance, wrapped in plastic wrap, and kept in the refrigerator or frozen. Use a fork to blend the blue cheese and butter, then season the mixture with a dash or two of Tabasco. Mold the mixture into a little log, wrap it in plastic, and refrigerate it. Double or triple this recipe, and you'll have plenty for another meal.

Season the steaks with salt and pepper. Grill, broil, or pan-sear the steaks to the desired degree of doneness. Set the steaks on a platter to rest for 7 minutes. Preheat a broiler. Slice the blue cheese butter into individual medallions of about ½-inch thickness. Place a medallion on each of the steaks and run the steaks under the broiler for about 30 seconds, to melt and lightly brown the topping. Serve immediately.

 A red Rioja

BEEF BRAISED IN BAROLO

Tony May, for decades one of New York's most outspoken ambassadors of fine Italian cooking, opened the elegant leather-upholstered San Domenico NY with a team of chefs who had worked at the Michelin three-star restaurant of the same name in Imola, Italy. The restaurant evolved and after nearly 20 years it closed and moved to a new location near Madison Park. Mr. May's daughter, Marisa May, helps run the restaurant. The chef, Odette Fada, interprets Italian food with great flair and finesse.

SERVES 4

2¼ pounds beef rump or top round in one piece, trimmed of fat

Salt and freshly ground black pepper

2 medium onions, peeled and quartered

2 carrots, peeled and quartered

3 celery stalks, quartered

2 thyme sprigs

6 rosemary sprigs

2 bay leaves

2 garlic cloves, crushed

½ teaspoon coriander seeds

1 bottle Barolo wine, plus additional if needed

½ cup all-purpose flour

2 tablespoons extra virgin olive oil

2 ounces pancetta, diced

Soft polenta or mashed potatoes, for serving

Place the meat in a large bowl, season with salt and pepper, and add the onions, carrots, celery, thyme, 2 sprigs of the rosemary, the bay leaves, garlic, and coriander. Add the wine, cover, and allow to marinate at room temperature for 2 hours, then refrigerate for at least 8 hours. Remove from the refrigerator 2 hours before cooking time.

Preheat the oven to 325 degrees. Remove the meat from the marinade, reserving the marinade. Dust meat with flour. Heat the oil in a 4- to 5-quart flameproof casserole over medium heat. Brown the meat on all sides. Take your time, turning the meat as each side browns. Remove the meat from pan, add the pancetta, and cook over medium-low heat until it starts to brown. Return the meat to the casserole along with any juices it has given off while resting, and the reserved marinade with all the vegetables and seasonings. Bring to a simmer, cover, and cook in the oven until fork-tender, about 3½ hours. It will shrink alarmingly, but it's so rich that you will still have enough.

This traditional Tuscan recipe needs the fresh rosemary—in the marinade, the casserole, and also on the plate—to come alive. The meat can be larded with herbs and pancetta before marinating.

Barolo, of course. Consider using the same wine for the marinade and at the table.

Remove the meat from the casserole and cover to keep warm. Remove and discard thyme and bay leaves from the casserole. Puree the cooking liquid and vegetables in a food processor or blender and return the sauce to the casserole.

Season to taste and reheat the sauce. If your sauce is too thick, add a little water or some more red wine. It should be the consistency of heavy cream. Reduce it if it's too thin. Slice the meat across the grain and arrange on a warm platter. Spoon sauce over meat and serve with polenta or mashed potatoes, with any extra sauce on the side. Garnish each portion with a remaining sprig of rosemary.

SHORT RIBS BRAISED IN RED WINE

DANIEL

Daniel Boulud's restaurant empire in New York covers all bases. Café Boulud is a comfortable Upper East Side restaurant that draws from well beyond the neighborhood for food inspired by France and beyond. DB Bistro Moderne in Midtown has a chic informality and Bar Boulud near Lincoln Center specializes in homemade charcuterie. But the jewel in the crown is Daniel, a room at once classic and modern, where a team of chefs turns food into art. Nonetheless, the chef-owner has not forgotten his background in a simple family restaurant kitchen in Lyon. And he does not hesitate to include lusty braised meats like short ribs on his exacting, exquisite menus.

3 bottles dry red wine

2 tablespoons canola or grapeseed oil

8 short ribs, about 8 pounds, cut in 24 pieces and trimmed of excess fat

Salt

1 teaspoon black peppercorns, crushed

All-purpose flour, for dredging

10 garlic cloves, peeled

8 large shallots, peeled, trimmed, split, rinsed, and dried

2 medium carrots, peeled and cut in 1-inch pieces

2 celery stalks, peeled and cut in 1-inch pieces

1 medium leek, white and light green parts, trimmed, rinsed, and coarsely chopped

6 flat-leaf parsley sprigs

2 thyme sprigs

2 bay leaves

2 tablespoons tomato paste

3 quarts unsalted beef stock

Freshly ground white pepper

Like many stewed meat dishes, this one benefits from being made a day in advance and reheated. The best plan is to cook the ribs, then refrigerate the whole affair overnight right in the pot so the fat on the surface will congeal and you can simply lift it off.

Pour the wine into a large saucepan set over medium heat. When the wine is hot, carefully set it aflame; stand back when you do this. When the flames die down, increase the heat and boil the wine until it is reduced by half to 4½ cups. Remove it from the heat.

Position a rack in the middle of the oven, and preheat the oven to 350 degrees.

Place a large, heavy casserole or Dutch oven on the stove, add the oil, and turn the heat to medium-high. Season the ribs all over with salt and crushed pepper. Lightly dust half the ribs with flour, then slip them into the pan and sear them on all sides, until well-browned. Transfer them to a plate and repeat this process with the rest of the ribs.

When all the ribs are brown, pour off all but a tablespoon of the fat in the pan and toss in the garlic, shallots, carrots, celery, leek, parsley, thyme, and bay leaves. Cook them over medium heat about 5 minutes, until they begin to color, then stir in the tomato paste. Cook another minute. Pour in the cooked wine and the stock, return the ribs to the pot, and bring everything to a boil. Cover the pot and place it in the oven to braise for about 2½ hours, until the ribs are fork-tender. While the meat is braising, lift the lid every 30 minutes or so to skim off excess fat.

Carefully transfer the meat to a warm serving platter that has a rim to catch the sauce. Tent the platter with foil to keep the meat warm.

On top of the stove, boil down the sauce until it has thickened and is reduced to about 4 cups. Pass it through a strainer (discard the solids), season it with salt and white pepper, spoon it over the meat, and serve.

A young, brawny Bordeaux from the Médoc, especially a Pauillac or a St. Julien

ROCK CANDY–GINGER SHORT RIBS

SHUN LEE PALACE

There is an enormous divide in New York between Chinatown Chinese restaurants and uptown Chinese palaces. Connoisseurs insist the food is best in Chinatown, assuming that unless the napkins are paper and the lighting is fluorescent, the food cannot be good. Michael Tong's restaurants—Shun Lee West and its café near Lincoln Center, and Shun Lee Palace on the East Side—expose this fallacy. Although his menus are filled with crowd-pleasers, it pays to seek out the less obvious, often seasonal, treasures, like a stir-fry of dried eels with Chinese chives, gray sole with ginger on a bed of crackling, deep-fried edible bones, and Rock Candy–Ginger Short Ribs. Dishes like these are served with elegance in plush surroundings.

SERVES 6

3 pounds beef short ribs, cut in 10 to 12 pieces, with bone

Salt and freshly ground black pepper

⅓ cup all-purpose flour

2 tablespoons peanut oil

⅓ cup dark soy sauce

⅓ cup light or thin soy sauce

2 cups *Shao Hsing* Chinese wine or dry sherry

1¼ cups sugar crystals or granulated sugar

1 piece star anise

1 cinnamon stick, broken in half

1 teaspoon black peppercorns

4 slices fresh ginger, each about ⅛ inch thick, peeled

2 whole scallions, trimmed

 A cabernet sauvignon, especially from Napa Valley

Dry the meat, season it with salt and ground pepper, and dredge it in the flour. Dust off any excess. Heat the oil in a heavy 4-quart casserole. Add the meat and sear it on all sides. You may have to do this in more than one batch.

Add the soy sauces, wine, sugar, star anise, cinnamon, peppercorns, ginger, and scallions. Bring to a simmer and stir in 8 cups of water. Bring to a fast boil, lower the heat to medium, cover the pan, and allow everything to cook for 2½ hours. Check from time to time to make sure that there is still enough liquid in the pot.

Carefully transfer the meat from the pan to a serving platter with a rim, and try to keep the bones attached. Pour the sauce into a bowl through a strainer (discard the solids), then return it to the casserole. Cook it until it has reduced to about 1½ cups and is syrupy. Pour the sauce over the meat and serve with steamed rice and Chinese broccoli.

 Dark Chinese soy sauce is thicker and less salty than thin or light (but not "lite") Chinese soy sauce.

CALF'S LIVER ALLA VENEZIANA

AL DI LA

An unpretentious, almost bare-bones room and exceptional Italian food that focuses on the cooking of the North around Venice have made Al Di La a magnet for lovers of Italian food, notwithstanding the wait for tables. The restaurant does not accept reservations. Among the first attention-getting spots to open on the now restaurant-heavy Fifth Avenue strip in Park Slope, Brooklyn, it attracts an audience far beyond its neighborhood precinct. But success has not gone to its head. It has maintained its local popularity as a family-friendly place for groups with children in tow.

SERVES 4

4 pieces calf's liver, each 4 to 5 ounces, cut ¾ inch thick

6 tablespoons unsalted butter

4 medium onions, peeled, halved, and sliced ⅛ inch thick

4 bay leaves, preferably fresh

Salt and freshly ground black pepper

¼ cup extra virgin olive oil

Leaves from 1 bunch fresh sage

1 cup chicken stock

1 teaspoon aged balsamic vinegar, at least 10 years old

A moscato giallo, a sweet white wine with high acidity. A red wine from the Veneto, such as a merlot, would pair nicely with the dish, too.

Trim the liver of any veins and outer membrane. Line a platter with paper towel and place the slices on it. Cover with another sheet of paper towel.

Melt 3 tablespoons of the butter in a large skillet, preferably nonstick, that can accommodate the liver in a single layer. Add the onions and bay leaves and cook over low heat, stirring frequently, until the onions become meltingly soft and golden, at least 15 minutes. Stir up any browned bits from the pan as you go. Transfer the onions to a smaller pan and remove the bay leaves. Wipe out the skillet.

Season the liver with salt and pepper. Heat the oil in the skillet and when it's hot, add the sage leaves. Stir-fry them briefly until they begin to crisp, and remove them to a plate. Add the liver and sear it over medium heat until it's browned but still rare in the middle, about 3 minutes per side. Remove the liver from the pan and pour off any excess oil. Add the remaining 3 tablespoons of butter to the pan and return the liver to the pan. Cook over medium heat about 5 minutes, basting the liver, until it becomes nicely glazed and is cooked medium-rare to medium. Transfer the liver to a plate and cover loosely with a piece

This recipe, perhaps the ultimate liver and onions, is a classic on the Venetian table. The first step in the preparation, sautéing the onions, must be done slowly, over moderate heat. But the liver needs a quick sauté in a hot pan, so it will be seared but not overcooked.

of foil. Add the chicken stock to the pan and cook, stirring with a wooden spoon to scrape up any browned bits, until the sauce has reduced by half. Season to taste with salt and pepper and stir in the vinegar. Reheat the onions in the small pan, then divide them among 4 dinner plates. Slice the liver on the bias about 1 inch thick and arrange the slices on the onions. Spoon the sauce over the liver, scatter on the sage leaves, and serve.

ROAST BEEF HASH

SMITH & WOLLENSKY

There is no Smith and no Wollensky. But Alan Stillman, the restaurateur who created TGI Friday's, is never short on cleverness. Another of his restaurants, Maloney & Porcelli, is named for his lawyers. He also owns the Park Avenue Café, where the décor changes completely for each season, The Post House, and Quality Meats, with a butcher shop vibe. Smith & Wollensky is the steakhouse that drives the company, a place for a great red wine to go with that steak.

SERVES 4

2 baking potatoes, each about 8 ounces, peeled and cut in ½-inch dice

Salt

2 tablespoons unsalted butter

2 tablespoons vegetable oil

1 cup diced onion

½ cup diced green pepper

4 cups finely diced cooked roast beef, preferably the deckle meat (see note below), not the eye

Freshly ground black pepper

2 tablespoons bottled steak sauce

4 poached eggs, optional

Place the potatoes in a pot with well-salted water to cover, bring to a boil, and cook 5 minutes. Drain well.

Heat the butter and oil in a large skillet. Add the onion and green pepper and sauté over medium heat. When they have softened, fold in the potatoes and cook the mixture, stirring occasionally, until the vegetables are lightly browned, at least 20 minutes. Fold in the roast beef, season with salt and pepper, and add the steak sauce. Continue to sauté about 15 minutes, until the mixture starts to crisp. Serve with a poached egg on each portion, if desired.

 A zinfandel

If you do not have leftover roast beef, you can prepare the hash by first roasting to medium doneness a pound of meat from the rib section, preferably the top, or deckle, meat, the strip of meat that surrounds the eye of the rib.

RABBIT ALLA CACCIATORE

Babbo is the capital of the Batali-Bastianich restaurant empire. Occupying the premises that once housed the legendary Coach House in Greenwich Village, it offers a robust personality in a straightforward, bustling trattoria setting. Tables are always in demand for those whose appetites are ready for hearty, inventive Italian food, so Chef Mario Batali and his partner in wine, Joseph Bastianich, offer alternatives nearby: Lupa, a minimally furnished country-style spot that accepts no reservations; Otto, a vast pizzeria where the side dishes and the desserts demand as much attention as the thin-crusted pizzas; and Del Posto, a grand palace of Italian *alta cucina*. But Babbo, which means "daddy" in Italian, a name that was attached to the place because both partners had just become parents, is where Batali's skill and invention shine. "I love the idea of garden peas and carrots in a rabbit dish," he said.

SERVES 4 TO 6

2 whole rabbits, each about 3
  pounds

⅔ cup extra virgin olive oil

2 carrots, peeled and coarsely
  chopped

1 large onion, peeled and coarsely
  chopped

2 celery stalks, coarsely chopped

1 cup dry white wine

2 cups chicken stock or water,
  approximately

1 tablespoon fresh rosemary leaves,
  chopped

1 tablespoon fresh thyme leaves,
  chopped

Salt and freshly ground black
  pepper

1 cup Thumbelina or baby carrots,
  peeled

½ cup sugar snap peas, trimmed

1 small onion, peeled and minced

1 cup dry red wine

1 tablespoon capers, rinsed and
  drained

2 tablespoons anchovy paste

2 tablespoons tomato paste

1 (12-inch) baguette, sliced thin on
  the bias and lightly toasted

1 cup pea shoots

Remove the livers, kidneys, and hearts from the rabbits. Remove the thighs and rear legs from the rabbits and separate the legs from the thighs. Refrigerate the thighs and the innards. Remove the front legs from the rabbits. Cut the remaining rabbit carcasses in half just where the rib cages end, separating the front part of the rabbits from the loins. Carefully cut the tenderloins from the backbones, keeping the flap that extends from the tenderloins intact. This sounds complicated, but with the rabbits on your cutting board, it is easy to understand the business about the flaps. Refrigerate the tenderloins. Chop the rest of the carcasses into 3 pieces.

Heat 2 tablespoons of the oil in a large casserole. Add the rabbit carcass pieces and all the rabbit legs, and cook until well browned on all sides. You may have to do this in more than one batch. Remove the rabbit pieces, add the chopped carrots, onion, and celery, and cook until browned. Add the white wine. Return the carcass pieces and legs to the casserole and add enough water or chicken stock to barely cover the bones. Cover and cook over low heat for 2 hours. Strain through a fine sieve. Discard the vegetables and bones.

While the stock is cooking, place the 4 tenderloins on a work surface, spreading out the flaps. Season the flaps with the rosemary, thyme, salt, and pepper. Roll the flap around the tenderloin and tie with a piece of butcher's string. Refrigerate.

In a 3- to 4-quart flameproof casserole, heat 4 tablespoons of the olive oil over medium-high heat. Add the thigh pieces in a single layer and cook until brown on all sides, about 6 minutes. Add 2 cups of the strained rabbit stock, reduce the heat to low, cover the pan, and braise for 15 minutes. Remove the thighs from the casserole and reduce the sauce until it's the consistency of heavy cream.

Check the seasonings. Return the thighs to the casserole and set aside.

Heat a grill or a grill pan until hot. Add the tenderloin pieces and cook, turning, until browned on the outside and cooked to about medium in the center, 6 to 8 minutes. An instant-read thermometer will register about 135 degrees. Transfer the tenderloins to the casserole.

In a small sauté pan heat 2½ tablespoons of the oil. Briefly sauté the baby carrots and sugar snap peas. Set aside.

In a small sauté pan, heat the remaining oil until very hot. Add the minced onion, sauté briefly, then add the livers, kidneys, and hearts and sauté until browned. Add the red wine, capers, anchovy paste, and tomato paste. Cook until the wine has reduced and the mixture has thickened. Transfer to a food processor and pulse to get a coarse puree. Season with salt and pepper and spread on the baguette slices to make crostini.

Briefly reheat the rabbit thighs and tenderloins in the sauce. Remove the tenderloin pieces, remove the strings, and cut each piece in half at an angle. Arrange the rabbit thighs and tenderloins on a serving platter. Stir the carrots and sugar snaps into the sauce, fold in the pea shoots, heat gently, and when they wilt, spoon the sauce onto the platter over and around the rabbit. Serve garnished with the crostini.

A light Tuscan red like Morrelino di Scansano

SIDE DISHES

FINGERLING POTATO PUREE 190

GERMAN FRIED POTATOES 192

GOOSE FAT POTATOES 194

WHITE SHOEPEG CORN PUDDING 196

MUSHROOM KASHA 197

ROASTED MUSHROOMS 198

SAUTÉED ZUCCHINI WITH TOASTED ALMONDS
AND PECORINO 200

SPINACH GRATIN 203

BHINDI DO PIAZA, SAUTÉED OKRA 204

GRILLED EGGPLANT WITH GINGER-LIME SAUCE 205

FINGERLING POTATO PUREE

BOULEY

David Bouley's flagship restaurant is a moving target. It started on Duane Street near Greenwich Street, then moved to the corner of Duane and West Broadway. Now it has relocated to the corner of Duane and Hudson Streets and is in the kind of luxurious setting that chefs in France inherit instead of building from scratch, as Bouley has done. His other properties have also undergone change, with Danube becoming the somewhat more casual, brasserie-style Secession, and Bouley Bakery and Market moving to the former Bouley space on the corner of West Broadway. But no matter the location, Bouley, the restaurant, can be counted on to serve this silken, unconscionably buttery potato puree inspired by the French master, Joël Robuchon.

SERVES 2 TO 4

1 pound fingerling potatoes, preferably *ratte* (see tip, opposite), peeled

Salt

⅓ cup heavy cream

2 cups milk

½ tablespoon pistachio oil or another nut oil such as hazelnut

½ tablespoon extra virgin olive oil

4 tablespoons (½ stick) soft unsalted butter

1 roasted garlic clove, mashed (see tip)

Freshly ground white pepper

Cut the potatoes into ½-inch pieces, place in a pot of well-salted cold water, bring to a boil, and cook until just tender, 15 to 20 minutes. Drain and pass through a ricer. Return to the cooking pot and stir them slowly over low heat with a wooden spoon for about 5 minutes to evaporate the excess moisture and concentrate the potato flavor.

Mix the cream, milk, pistachio oil, and olive oil together in a small saucepan and heat until just under a simmer. Add this mixture slowly to the potatoes, stirring lightly, until the puree is smooth and very creamy.

Now pass the puree through a fine sieve—a tamis or a chinois is best—into the top of a double boiler or a bain-marie. Do this a little at a time, but quickly so you do not overwork the potatoes, which is likely to happen if you try to sieve them all at once. Fold in the butter and the roasted garlic and place over boiling water to keep warm. Place the wrapper from a stick of butter directly on top of the potatoes.

Just before serving, whip the potatoes with a whisk to smooth them, and check seasoning. Serve hot.

Two people could polish off the potatoes, especially if some fresh black truffles are shaved on the top, making Champagne or a rich white Burgundy the wine of choice. Otherwise, what to drink alongside depends on what accompanies the potatoes.

The best potato to use for this puree is the *ratte*, a French variety that some farmers now grow and sell in farmers markets. Other fingerling potatoes or even Yukon golds are also suitable.

To make roasted garlic, brush a head of garlic with olive oil, wrap it in foil, and place it in a 400-degree oven until the cloves are tender, 30 to 40 minutes. Peel and use as many cloves as needed and refrigerate the rest.

GERMAN FRIED POTATOES

PETER LUGER STEAK HOUSE

New York boasts a number of famous steak houses. Peter Luger Steak House, in Williamsburg, Brooklyn, is in a class by itself. A holdover from another era, it does not accept credit cards, offers an extremely limited menu, does not pride itself on its wines, and is still family-owned and -run. As for the prime beef that is butchered into its steaks, it is hand-selected daily from a number of purveyors. Peter Luger broils only the loin cuts—the short loin or porterhouse—no rib-eye, and the steaks are glossed with butter as they come to the table. It would be next to impossible to reproduce one of the steaks at home, but the potatoes can be done, to serve with the best steak you can find. Try them with City Hall's Delmonico Steak with Maytag blue cheese, page 173.

SERVES 4 TO 6

5 medium-large Idaho potatoes

3 cups vegetable oil

1 large Spanish onion, peeled and diced

Salt

Pinch paprika

6 tablespoons unsalted butter

Freshly ground white pepper

> The preliminary frying is the first step in making classic french fries. The second step is to refry the potatoes until they are brown.
>
> The potatoes and onions can be served as soon as they are browned, without reheating.

This recipe is accomplished in three stages, and all but the final 10 minutes can be prepared in advance.

Peel the potatoes and cut them in ½-inch thick sticks as for french fries. As they're cut, put them in a bowl of cold water so they do not discolor. In a deep-fryer, a deep sauté pan, or a wok, heat the 3 cups of oil until very hot. While the oil is heating, take the potatoes out of the water and spread them on several layers of paper towel to dry thoroughly. When the oil is hot, about 375 degrees, fry the potatoes until they're barely colored, 4 to 5 minutes. It's best to do this in batches; three should work well. Use a skimmer to drain the potatoes as they are done and transfer them to paper towels.

When all the potatoes are fried, spoon 3 tablespoons of the oil into a large skillet and sauté the onion over medium heat, stirring frequently. Dust them with a little salt and paprika as they fry. When they're soft and golden, remove them.

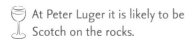 At Peter Luger it is likely to be Scotch on the rocks.

When the potatoes have cooled, place them on a cutting board, all facing in one direction, and cut them into dice. Melt the butter in a large skillet. Fry the potatoes, stirring from time to time, for 5 minutes or so, until they are nicely browned. Fold in the onion, 1 teaspoon of salt, and some pepper, and fry another few minutes until everything is browned. Transfer the mixture to a 10-inch pie pan or baking dish. Set it aside until just before serving.

Preheat the oven to 400 degrees. Place the potatoes in the oven for 10 minutes, then serve.

GOOSE FAT POTATOES

> *Strip House, a play on words,* is a steak house designed to have a rather "louche" and playful bordello look; lots of red, and walls lined with vintage French photos of strippers set the tone. The success of Strip House has led the Glazier Group, which also owns Michael Jordan's The Steakhouse NYC in Grand Central Terminal, to branch out to other cities. There are several cuts of steak on the menu, along with veal, chicken, and seafood. And as well as creamed spinach and french fries, the star of the side dishes are the Goose Fat Potatoes that Peter Glazier wanted on the menu, and which John Schenk interprets. Dessert at any table is bound to include the famous twelve-layer chocolate cake.

Serves 4

3 cups goose or duck fat
(sold in fancy food shops,
see tip, page 155)

5 fresh rosemary sprigs

5 fresh thyme sprigs

½ tablespoon whole black
peppercorns

8 garlic cloves

Kosher salt

3 large Idaho potatoes, peeled
and cut in ½-inch dice

½ tablespoon chopped thyme

½ tablespoon chopped rosemary

Freshly ground black pepper

1 tablespoon minced flat-leaf
parsley

Preheat the oven to 400 degrees.

Bring fat to a simmer in a 3-quart saucepan. Place rosemary and thyme sprigs, peppercorns, and 6 of the garlic cloves, split, in a 12-inch length of cheesecloth. Tie securely and place in the fat. Season the fat with salt. Add the potatoes and cook at a steady simmer until potatoes are tender but still hold their shape, about 10 minutes.

Use a slotted spoon to transfer the potatoes to a bowl, draining them well. Discard the cheese cloth package. Strain the fat and refrigerate it. Fold the chopped thyme and rosemary into the potatoes and season them to taste with salt and pepper. Pack the potatoes into 4 (4-ounce) cupcake molds or in a muffin tin. Bake 20 minutes, until they start to brown. Remove pan from oven, allow to cool 30 minutes, then refrigerate at least 4 hours or overnight.

Preheat the oven to 450 degrees.

Line a baking sheet with parchment and brush with a little of the reserved fat. Run a knife around the inside of the molds, invert molds onto the parchment, and tap so the

The recipe can also be prepared with olive oil or half olive oil and half clarified butter. Another way to reheat the potatoes and crisp them is by deep-frying. Remove the chilled potato cakes from the molds and set in a deep saucepan that will hold them in a single layer. Heat goose or duck fat—you can use the fat reserved from the first cooking, it might be just enough—and carefully pour it over the potatoes. Bring to a simmer and cook until the potato cakes are crisp and golden. Remove the cakes with a slotted spoon or a spatula, drain them briefly, then serve.

What to drink with goose fat potatoes depends on what main course they accompany. With a steak, a good California cabernet sauvignon is always on target, or a sturdy pinot noir.

potatoes are released onto the parchment. Brush with a little of the fat. Mince the remaining 2 garlic cloves and place on top of the potato mounds. Place potatoes in the oven and bake about 20 minutes, until lightly browned. Garnish with parsley and serve.

WHITE SHOEPEG CORN PUDDING

Barbecue has certainly taken hold in New York. Hill Country is one of several fairly new pit-smoking restaurants. Here it's a combination restaurant and market, without waiter service, where customers select their slabs of ribs and smoky slices of brisket and pork shoulder, along with sides and drinks, from a counter, fast-food style. Among the fairly typical list of side dishes is this corn pudding made with white corn. To make it a year-round dish, the restaurant's shoepeg corn, a variety of white corn, is frozen. Yours can be, too, though fresh corn makes a delicious option in summer.

SERVES 6 TO 8

2 tablespoons unsalted butter

4 cups (about 28 ounces) frozen white corn kernels

1 cup heavy cream

1 large egg

½ teaspoon granulated sugar

Sea salt and freshly ground white pepper

Pinch cayenne

½ teaspoon ground nutmeg

2 tablespoons chopped fresh chives

½ cup finely chopped shallots

½ cup shredded mild cheddar cheese

½ cup shredded Monterey Jack

When fresh corn is in season, white corn kernels, stripped from the cobs can replace frozen. You will need 8 to 10 ears for 4 cups of kernels.

Preheat the oven to 350 degrees. Use ½ tablespoon of the butter to grease a shallow 9-inch square baking dish or one about 11 by 7 inches.

Bring 2 quarts of salted water to a boil in a large pot. Cook the corn until tender, about 3 minutes, and drain. Reserve 1 cup of the corn. Place the remaining corn in a food processor. Add the cream and puree until smooth. Add the egg and pulse until completely combined. Add sugar, sea salt, white pepper, cayenne, nutmeg, and chives. Blend well, pour in a large bowl and set aside.

Melt the remaining butter in a medium-size skillet. Add the shallots and sauté over medium heat until they begin to color. Stir in the reserved cup of corn and just heat through, mixing with the shallots. Add to the corn puree and stir in the cheeses.

Pour into the baking dish and place it in a larger baking pan. Pour hot water into the large pan to come halfway up the sides of the baking dish. Carefully place the baking pan in the oven and bake until the pudding is set and golden on top, about 1 hour. Serve hot or at room temperature.

A Doppel-Bock or Oktoberfest beer from Germany, in keeping with the German heritage of Texas barbecue.

MUSHROOM KASHA

New York has several Russian communities, the most famous of which is Brighton Beach, Brooklyn, where the avenues are lined with boisterous Russian night-club restaurants. But in Manhattan's Theater District, an elaborate double town house furnished with Imperial Russian accessories is the setting for New York's most elegant Russian restaurant. From the cozy ground floor bar, to the dining room with its golden pear tree centerpiece, to the second floor decorated with ballet costumes, stepping into Firebird is like entering a Fabergé egg. The food is Russian, with vodka and caviar, hors d'oeuvre plates called zakuski, and classics like beef Stroganoff, borscht, chicken Kiev, and shashlik. But the menu also offers an array of contemporary dishes as well, such as lobster bisque, filet mignon, and hot-smoked salmon, for those who want a Russian atmosphere but may not want St. Petersburg on the plate.

SERVES 4

1¼ cups chicken stock

Salt and freshly ground black pepper

1 cup whole buckwheat groats (kasha)

2 tablespoons soft unsalted butter

1 tablespoon extra virgin olive oil

6 ounces button mushrooms, trimmed and coarsely chopped

2 tablespoons sour cream

1 teaspoon minced chives

If desired, wild mushrooms such as chanterelles or morels can be used instead of white button mushrooms.

Bring the chicken stock to a boil in a 2-quart saucepan. Season it well with salt and pepper, stir in the kasha, cover the pan, and set it aside off the heat for 15 to 20 minutes, until the stock has been absorbed and the kasha is tender.

While the kasha is steeping, heat 1 tablespoon of the butter with the olive oil in a skillet. Add the mushrooms and cook, stirring, over medium heat, until they are tender, have given up their liquid, and the liquid has evaporated. Season to taste with salt and pepper and fold in the sour cream and chives.

When the kasha is ready, toss it with a fork, then fold in the remaining tablespoon of the butter. Fold in the mushroom mixture and serve.

 A rich red wine

ROASTED MUSHROOMS

FAIRWAY STEAKHOUSE

A market-restaurant is a natural fit. In Sheepshead Bay, Brooklyn, clam bars share the space with fish markets; the Old Homestead sells its steaks retail; and many bakeries have café tables for those seeking instant gratification. For three years the second floor at the original Fairway market on the Upper West Side has housed a café for breakfast and lunch. Now, at dinner, it becomes a steakhouse with a straightforward menu offering slabs of prime meat, plus a few chicken, fish, and pasta selections, and a roster of appealing appetizers, side dishes, and desserts. Mitchel London, an uncompromising culinary wizard who once cooked for Mayor Ed Koch at Gracie Mansion, is at the stove. His roasted mushrooms are a good partner for the rib eye.

2 garlic cloves

½ bunch flat-leaf parsley

¼ cup plus 1 tablespoon extra virgin olive oil

½ pound oyster mushrooms

½ pound chanterelle mushrooms

½ pound shiitake mushrooms

2 tablespoons clarified butter

Sea salt and freshly ground black pepper

The selection of mushrooms is pretty basic, and if there are other, more exotic varieties like morels, hedgehogs, or bluefoots in the market, they can be added to or used instead of the list in the recipe.

Turn on the food processor and toss the garlic in through the feed tube. When it's finely chopped, scrape down the sides of the work bowl, add the parsley, and process until finely chopped. With the machine running, pour in ¼ cup of the oil in a thin stream. Scrape down the sides of the bowl, then pulse to make a fairly fine mixture but one that's got some texture. You do not want a smooth puree. Set the mixture aside.

Preheat the oven to 475 degrees.

Trim the mushrooms: Separate the oyster mushrooms and leave only about ½ inch of stem; scrape and trim the stems of the chanterelles; and discard the stems of the shiitakes. Halve or quarter the shiitake caps to make fairly uniform pieces.

Heat the clarified butter and remaining tablespoon of olive oil in a large skillet (about 14 inches) that can hold all the mushrooms. Alternatively, you can divide everything between two pans. Add the mushrooms and toss over high heat 3 to 4 minutes, until they wilt. Transfer the mushrooms to a shallow roasting pan and roast in the oven for 15 minutes.

Remove the mushrooms from the oven and toss with the parsley mixture. Season with salt and pepper and serve.

A robust red wine with a nice amount of bottle age that will also complement your steak

SAUTÉED ZUCCHINI WITH TOASTED ALMONDS AND PECORINO

RED CAT

Just about every neighborhood in New York today boasts at least one restaurant that counts on a loyal local clientele but, because the food is a good notch above everyday, also attracts visitors from far and wide. The Red Cat in Chelsea is just such place, serving forthright Mediterranean-style cooking in a simple whitewashed room. Its success has led the owner, chef Jimmy Bradley, to open The Harrison in TriBeCa.

SERVES 4

¼ cup extra virgin olive oil

½ cup sliced almonds

1½ pounds zucchini, trimmed and cut in julienne

Salt and freshly ground black pepper

3 ounces Pecorino Romano cheese, shaved in thin slices

Be careful not to overcook the zucchini. It should still be slightly crisp so it does not give off much liquid as it cools.

Use a vegetable peeler to shave the cheese.

Heat the oil in a large skillet. Add the almonds and fry until golden. Use a slotted spoon to scoop out the almonds, leaving the oil in the pan. Add the zucchini and stir-fry about 30 seconds, long enough to warm it and coat it with the oil without really cooking it. Remove the pan from the heat. Season the zucchini with salt and pepper. Return the pan to the heat to rewarm, transfer the zucchini to a warm serving dish, top with the cheese and almonds and serve.

 A dry Italian white such as Gavi di Gavi

SPINACH GRATIN

Peter Hoffman, the chef and owner of Savoy, a two-story spot on a back-street in SoHo, is a farmer's chef. He consults the calendar and features produce only when it is in season. "At one time a fine restaurant was one that served asparagus and raspberries in December," he once said. "Today it is one that doesn't." And he refuses to compromise. The main floor of his sleek yet cozy wood-paneled restaurant is a bar and lounge. Upstairs, the dining room features a wood-burning fireplace, which he uses frequently to roast fish, meats, poultry, and vegetables.

SERVES 4

2½ tablespoons extra virgin olive oil
1 garlic clove, sliced
¾ cup *panko* (Japanese white bread crumbs)
½ teaspoon fennel seeds
4 tablespoons (½ stick) unsalted butter
2 pounds fresh spinach, stemmed and rinsed thoroughly
2 tablespoons flour
1¼ cups milk, scalded
2 eggs, beaten
Salt and freshly ground black pepper

With the gratin alone, a fruity California gewürztraminer

Try to find good, locally grown spinach. Other greens, such as kale or Swiss chard, can be used in place of spinach.

Heat 2 tablespoons of the oil in a small skillet. Add the garlic and cook a few minutes, until it starts to brown. Remove and discard the garlic and stir in the panko. Sauté until they're lightly toasted. Stir in the fennel seeds and set the crumbs aside.

Preheat the oven to 375 degrees. Use the remaining half tablespoon oil to grease a 4-cup baking dish.

Heat 2 tablespoons of the butter in a large skillet. Add the spinach and cook, stirring, over high heat about a minute just until it starts to wilt. Remove from the heat and set aside.

Melt the remaining butter in a 2-quart saucepan. Whisk in the flour, cook a few minutes, then whisk in the milk. Simmer a few minutes until this white sauce has thickened. Remove from the heat. Beat a little of this mixture into the eggs, then whisk the eggs back into the sauce. Season with salt and pepper.

Remove the spinach from the skillet, draining it thoroughly, and place on a cutting board. Chop roughly. Fold the spinach into the sauce. Taste and correct seasoning. Transfer to the baking dish, top with the crumbs, and bake 20 to 25 minutes, until lightly browned on top.

BHINDI DO PIAZA, SAUTÉED OKRA

TAMARIND

Sixth Street in the East Village, Lexington Avenue in the 20s, and Jackson Heights, Queens, are New York's major low-price Indian restaurant quarters. There are Indian restaurants in Midtown too, but they tend to be maharajah-style palaces. Tamarind, in the Flatiron district, with its clean, monochromatic, modern decor and fine Indian art, is in a class by itself. Although the food is clearly rooted in the Indian idiom, it ventures beyond the typical dishes such as chicken tikka masala and tandoori chicken. Giant filled *dosa* pancakes, spiced lamb sandwiches on Indian bread, tandoori lobster tails, and beans with coconut and curry leaves define what the restaurant calls modern Indian cooking. There is a little tea-and-snacks café next door.

SERVES 4 TO 6

6 tablespoons vegetable oil
1 tablespoon cumin seeds
1 pound okra, trimmed and sliced ½ inch thick
2 large onions, peeled and chopped
4 garlic cloves, chopped
1 tablespoon minced fresh ginger
1 jalapeño chile, stemmed, seeded, and minced
½ tablespoon ground coriander
½ tablespoon chile powder
½ tablespoon turmeric
Salt
1 pound ripe tomatoes, chopped
½ tablespoon *amchoor* (mango powder), optional
2 tablespoons cilantro leaves

 A chardonnay or a pinot noir

Heat 3 tablespoons of the oil in a large skillet. Add the cumin seeds, and when they crackle, toss in the okra and cook over high heat, stirring, until the okra starts to brown, about 5 minutes. Remove the okra from the skillet and set it aside.

Add the remaining 3 tablespoons of oil, half the onions, and the garlic to the skillet. Cook until lightly browned, then stir in the ginger, jalapeño, ground coriander, chile powder, and turmeric. Add 1 teaspoon salt, or to taste. Add the tomatoes and *amchoor,* if using, and cook, stirring, until the ingredients are softened and cling together. Return the okra to the pan, along with the remaining onions. Cook briefly, then fold in half of the cilantro. Check seasoning and serve with the remaining cilantro sprinkled on top.

> Purchase okra with bright green pods, the smaller the better. Baby okra does not have to be sliced for this recipe.
> Mango powder is available in Indian grocery stores.

GRILLED EGGPLANT WITH GINGER-LIME SAUCE

For many years there were no Vietnamese restaurants in Manhattan. Now there are many, and fine ones, too, from little spots that specialize in the restorative and ubiquitous soup, pho, to more elaborate fare. Stephen Duong's Vietnamese restaurants are a stylish group: Cyclo in the East Village, Nam in TriBeCa, and O Mai in Chelsea. Of the three, Nam, in a TriBeCa building with stately columns out front, is the most alluring. The almost bare white interior glows with warm light, softened with gauzy curtains and punctuated with discreet black- and-white photos of old Hanoi. Vietnamese women do the cooking, often producing family recipes and homestyle dishes. Their cuisine blends the richness of China with the perfumed freshness of Southeast Asia.

SERVES 4

⅓ cup extra virgin olive oil

1 scallion, minced

1 tablespoon Vietnamese or Thai fish sauce

1 tablespoon sugar

1 tablespoon lime juice

1 garlic clove, finely minced

1 small fresh red chile, stemmed, seeded, and minced, or to taste

1 (1-inch) piece fresh ginger, peeled and thinly sliced

3 teaspoons minced cilantro leaves

4 slender Japanese eggplants, each about 8 ounces

> Regular eggplant can be used instead of the slender Asian variety, but the skin will not be as tender and it may need a couple more minutes on the grill.

Heat the oil until very hot in a small saucepan. Remove from the heat, add the scallion, stir, and set aside.

Combine the fish sauce, sugar, lime juice, garlic, chile, ginger, and 2 teaspoons of the cilantro in a blender. Blend until well combined but only until the ginger is minced, not pureed. Set aside.

Trim the stems from the eggplants and slice each in half lengthwise. Pare off a wide strip of the skin lengthwise, with a vegetable peeler. Place the eggplants in a bowl and massage with the reserved scallion oil.

Preheat a grill to medium-hot. Grill the eggplant halves about 2 minutes on each side, until nicely seared and tender. Remove the eggplant from the grill and cut into 1-inch chunks. Arrange in a shallow serving dish, pour the sauce over it, toss lightly, sprinkle with the remaining cilantro, and serve.

 A dry Alsatian riesling

DESSERTS

CRÈME BRÛLÉE

Sirio Maccioni, the quintessential restaurateur, has made Le Cirque the ultimate of New York restaurants, and perhaps the world's most famous restaurant. It is on the "must list" for celebrities in society, politics, fashion, and entertainment. It survived a move from East 65th Street to the landmark Villard Houses at the New York Palace as Le Cirque 2000. Now, having moved again to East 58th Street, it boasts a vast, gleaming kitchen and brilliantly dazzling decor by Adam Tihany. The menu is French-Italian but the chefs also dote on the clientele, and offer everything from pristine grilled fish to elaborate pot-au-feu and bouillabaisse. Maccioni's three sons participate in running Le Cirque, the Osteria del Circo across town, and branches of Le Cirque and Circo in Las Vegas and Mexico. Travel to France or Italy, and chances are some of the best restaurants will feature Crème Brûlée Le Cirque on their menus, just as Paul Bocuse does.

1 quart heavy cream
1 Tahitian vanilla bean, halved
  lengthwise, seeds scraped out
  and reserved
½ cup granulated sugar
8 egg yolks
8 tablespoons light brown sugar

A rich French Sauternes

Shallow fluted oval white
porcelain ramekins are the
classic dishes for serving crème
brûlée. But Le Cirque also serves
minis, in small 2-ounce glass cups.

Because the custards can
be prepared in advance and
refrigerated until just before
serving, they are excellent to
consider when entertaining.

Preheat the oven to 250 degrees.

Place the cream, vanilla seeds, and granulated sugar in a
saucepan. Place over low heat and cook until just warm to
the touch, stirring occasionally until the sugar dissolves.

Place egg yolks in a large mixing bowl. Whisk in a tablespoon or two of the warm cream, then lightly whisk in the
remaining cream. Pour the mixture through a fine sieve or
a chinois into a clean bowl, pressing as much vanilla as
possible through the sieve.

Place 8 shallow 4-ounce ramekins in 1 or 2 rimmed baking
sheets or roasting pans, whichever will accommodate
them. Ladle the cream mixture into the ramekins, stirring
it well so the vanilla is evenly distributed. Pour about
½ inch of hot water into the pans. Bake 1 hour and 15
minutes, rotating the pans once so the custards bake
evenly, until the custards look firm and just tremble
slightly in the middle. Allow to cool, then refrigerate at
least 3 hours or up to 2 days.

To serve, sprinkle the cold custards with brown sugar,
coating the tops completely. Caramelize the sugar with a
kitchen torch held about 1½ inches from the surface. Alternatively, the custards can be caramelized under a broiler,
although it is best to do this one at a time, so they are evenly
browned. Take care that the sugar does not burn.

Allow to cool briefly so the surface crisps, then serve.

PUMPKIN GENOISE WITH PEARS
IN RED WINE

CORTON

> *Back in the late 1980s,* when TriBeCa was just beginning to become a dining and nightlife destination, Drew Nieporent, restaurateur extraordinaire, cobbled together a partnership and raised enough money to open Montrachet. It never wavered from its original concept, to offer fine American food with a French accent, and French wine discoveries to accompany it, all at a reasonable price. Nieporent closed Montrachet for more than a year, reopening it as Corton, with Paul Liebrandt, a creative English chef in the kitchen and Robert Truitt as pastry chef.

SERVES 8

1 tablespoon soft unsalted butter

1⅓ cups flour, plus more for pan

½ teaspoon baking soda

1½ cups (12 ounces) squash or
    pumpkin puree

⅔ cup turbinado sugar

½ teaspoon salt

½ cup extra virgin olive oil

2 large eggs

⅓ cup dark beer

2 cups dry red wine

½ cup granulated sugar

2 tablespoons pear *eau de vie*

2 ripe pears, peeled, cored, and
    diced

⅔ cup heavy cream, whipped

Pear sorbet for serving, optional

8 fresh thyme sprigs

Preheat the oven to 350 degrees. Butter a 9-inch round cake pan, preferably with a removable bottom. Fit a round of parchment paper into the bottom, butter the paper, and dust the pan with flour.

Whisk the flour and baking soda together in a small bowl.

Place the squash, sugar, salt, olive oil, eggs, and beer in a bowl and beat with an electric mixer until smooth. Fold in the flour mixture. Spread the batter in the pan and bake just until the cake is springy to the touch, about 30 minutes. Cool for 10 minutes in the pan, then invert the cake onto a rack and peel off the paper. Continue cooling.

While the cake, is cooling place the wine and granulated sugar in a saucepan and cook until it is reduced to about 1¼ cups and has become syrupy. Add half of the *eau de vie* and the diced pears. Refrigerate.

Whip the cream and fold in the remaining *eau de vie*. Refrigerate.

To serve, cut the cake in wedges and spoon some of the pears in red wine over and around each portion. Top with whipped cream and, if desired, place a small scoop of pear sorbet alongside. Garnish each serving with a sprig of thyme.

You can cook and puree butternut squash, acorn squash, or pumpkin yourself or use canned or frozen versions. But the puree must be unseasoned.

The dessert is not too sweet and can handle a late-harvest muscadelle from Gaillac in southwestern France.

FROZEN TANGERINE SOUFFLÉ WITH BURNT TANGERINE AND VANILLA CARAMEL

TOCQUEVILLE

> *Tocqueville, named for the Frenchman who toured America* in the early nineteenth century and wrote about it, started off in very modest fashion as a small yet elegant restaurant; subsequently it moved to a far grander setting a few doors down the block. The food is inventive and is often seasoned with touches of Asia. Marco Moreira, the chef, who owns the restaurant with his wife, Jo-Ann Makovitzky, finds the allure of Japan almost irresistible. In fact, they have turned the former premises of Tocqueville into a Japanese restaurant, 15 East.

SERVES 8

4 cups fresh, frozen, or bottled tangerine juice

2 vanilla beans, halved lengthwise, seeds scraped out

3 large eggs, at room temperature, separated

2¾ cups granulated sugar

1½ cups heavy cream

4 tangerines or navel oranges, in segments, for garnish

Place the tangerine juice and vanilla bean seeds in a saucepan and simmer until the juice has reduced to 1 cup. Set aside to cool.

Place the egg yolks in a large bowl and beat with an electric mixer, preferably a standing mixer, gradually adding ¼ cup of the sugar, until the volume has doubled and the mixture has become very light and creamy, 5 to 7 minutes. Gently stir in half of the reduced tangerine juice and reserve.

In a clean bowl with a clean beater, whip the egg whites at medium speed until very softly peaked. Gradually add ½ cup of the sugar and whip until stiffly peaked, about 4 minutes. In a separate bowl, whip the heavy cream until almost stiffly peaked. Carefully fold the egg yolk mixture into the whites. Fold in the whipped cream.

Place the mixture in a 10-cup soufflé dish. Cover with plastic wrap. Freeze for at least 6 hours or overnight.

To prepare the sauce, place the remaining 2 cups of sugar in a 4-quart saucepan, preferably one that is not too deep. Add ½ cup water and stir to moisten the sugar. Place over medium-high heat and cook, swirling the pan from time to

This frozen soufflé is actually a kind of short-cut ice cream, made without churning, called a semifreddo.

This dessert is made with uncooked eggs. Using organic eggs will reduce any risk of safety. And those who need more assurance should purchase pasteurized yolks and whites, which are now sold in containers, even in supermarkets.

time, until the sugar melts and turns a medium caramel color, about 10 minutes. While the sugar is caramelizing, place the remaining reduced tangerine juice in a small pan and heat it to a simmer. Remove it from the heat, and when the sugar has caramelized, pour the warm juice into the pan but stand back because it may spatter. Whisk the sauce gently until the bubbles subside. Remove from heat and allow to cool to room temperature.

Shortly before serving, place the soufflé in the refrigerator to temper it. Serve it with the sauce. Garnish each plate with fresh tangerine or orange segments.

A Bordelais dessert wine, preferably a Sauternes

WHITE SESAME MOUSSE

KAI

> *This cool green and black granite second-floor enclave* over a tea shop has to be a destination. It serves lunch, tea, and, for dinner, elegant and inventive kaiseki Japanese menus. As with most kaiseki menus, exquisite presentation is the rule. And so are surprises, like a tantalizing bit of seasonal herb here, or an unusual flavor there. Delicately nutty white sesame paste gives this chilled dessert mousse a unique personality. Kai is owned by the Japanese tea company, Ito En, whose shop is downstairs.

SERVES 4 TO 6

¼ cup Japanese white sesame paste (sold in Asian markets)

1⅓ cups whole milk

½ cup sugar

¼ teaspoon salt

1 packet unflavored gelatin (1 tablespoon)

1 cup heavy cream

⅓ cup warm chocolate sauce, optional

1 tablespoon toasted white sesame seeds

Japanese sesame paste is like natural peanut butter. It separates. Before using it, stir it thoroughly to reincorporate the oil.

In a 1-quart saucepan, whisk the sesame paste into the milk until well-blended. Stir in the sugar and salt and ½ cup of water. Bring to a simmer, whisking constantly. Remove from the heat. Soften the gelatin in ½ cup of cold water in a small dish, and whisk it into the milk and sesame mixture. Return to the heat very briefly, whisk, then remove. Transfer the mixture to a medium metal bowl and set the bowl in a larger bowl of ice water so it can chill. Whisk it from time to time as it cools.

When the mixture has cooled and started to thicken, whip the cream. Gradually fold the whipped cream into the sesame mixture until it is smoothly incorporated. Spoon the mixture into 4 to 6 stemmed goblets, cover each with plastic wrap, and refrigerate at least 6 hours.

To serve, drizzle a little warm chocolate sauce on top of each portion, then sprinkle with sesame seeds. The sauce can be omitted and just the sesame seeds used, if desired.

A late-harvest Malvasia

CHEESECAKE

CARNEGIE DELI

A tourist magnet in Midtown, a Broadway icon, and a landmark of sorts, the Carnegie Deli, named for nearby Carnegie Hall, is an abiding representative of New York's Jewish culture. Known for its sandwiches piled high with corned beef and pastrami as much as for its brusque waiters, it is a place to go for the bustling scene first, then for the food. You do not need a recipe to make one of those sandwiches. You just need to buy enough sliced meat.
But the classic New York cheesecake is another story. You can bake it and, as your waiter might say, "Enjoy!"

9 tablespoons soft unsalted butter

½ cup sifted confectioners' sugar, plus more for dusting

3 eggs

2¾ cups all-purpose flour

½ teaspoon salt

2 pounds cream cheese, softened

1¼ cups granulated sugar

1 teaspoon vanilla extract

2 tablespoons lemon juice

½ cup sour cream

 A cuppa coffee

The rather unorthodox baking method assures that the top of the cake and the pastry will brown but that the cake will not crack or sink from overbaking.

Beat the butter in an electric mixer. Beat in ½ cup of the confectioners' sugar until smooth. Beat in 1 egg. Whisk 2 cups of the flour with the salt. Stir the flour mixture into the butter mixture and beat just until a soft dough forms. Divide it in half. Roll one half into a circle to fit in the bottom of an 8-inch springform pan. Roll the remaining dough into a rectangle about 6 by 12 inches. Cut it in half lengthwise. Place the strips in the pan to line the sides, pressing the seams together. Trim to make a smooth edge on top. Prick the bottom. Refrigerate while the oven is preheating.

Preheat the oven to 425 degrees.

Line the pastry-filled pan with foil and weight with dry beans or pastry weights. Place in the oven and bake about 10 minutes. Remove the foil and continue baking until the pastry has just started to color, another 6 to 8 minutes. Remove from the oven and increase the temperature to 475 degrees.

Beat the cream cheese with the granulated sugar. Beat in the remaining ¾ cup of flour, the remaining 2 eggs, the vanilla, lemon juice, and sour cream. Pour into the pastry shell, place in the oven, and bake about 20 minutes, until the top is golden. Remove cake from the oven. Lower temperature to 350 degrees. Allow the cake to sit for 20 minutes. Return the cake to the oven and continue baking it for about 25 minutes, until the top starts to puff. Set the cake aside at room temperature for about 5 hours, then refrigerate until cold.

Remove cake from refrigerator at least 1 hour before serving and sift a layer of confectioners' sugar on top.

BITTERSWEET CHOCOLATE SOUFFLÉ

PAYARD BISTRO

François Payard, from a family of pastry chefs in Nice, France, worked in some of New York's best kitchens and made his reputation before venturing out on his own. His pastry shop–tea room–bistro on the Upper East Side has a regular following for morning croissants, light café fare, a bistro lunch at midday, and cocktails and dinner in the evening. The coffee and wine bar is always crowded. The shop and two-story restaurant have a traditional look, suggesting Art Nouveau. But look again. You may notice that some of the light fixtures are designed like whisks.

SERVES 8

6 tablespoons soft unsalted butter

⅓ cup plus 2 tablespoons sugar

7 ounces high-quality bittersweet chocolate, chopped

1 tablespoon crème fraîche

4 eggs, separated, at room temperature

3 egg whites, at room temperature

½ teaspoon cream of tartar

Unsweetened whipped cream, optional

 A Monbazillac, or a Sauternes

Using about 1½ tablespoons of the butter, generously brush the insides of 8 (6-ounce) ramekins with butter. Place them in the freezer and chill for 15 minutes. Brush with another 1½ tablespoons of the butter. Use the 2 tablespoons of the sugar to coat the insides of the ramekins. Tap out any excess. Place the ramekins in the refrigerator.

Place remaining 3 tablespoons of butter and the chocolate in a 1-quart metal bowl over simmering water in a saucepan, or in the top of a double boiler. Melt, stirring occasionally, until smooth. Whisk in the crème fraîche. Transfer mixture to a 4-quart bowl, and set aside to cool.

Preheat the oven to 350 degrees.

Whisk the 4 egg yolks into cooled chocolate mixture. Using an electric mixer, beat the 7 egg whites at low speed until foamy. Add the cream of tartar and beat at medium speed until softly peaked. Gradually add the remaining ⅓ cup of sugar and beat at medium-high speed until stiffly peaked but still glossy. Using a large rubber spatula, fold a scoop of the beaten whites thoroughly into the chocolate mixture. Gently fold in remaining whites.

To obtain the maximum volume from the egg whites, make sure they are at room temperature before beating, and incorporate them into the batter very gradually.

Carefully spoon the mixture into the ramekins, filling them three-quarters full. Take a piece of paper towel and wipe the exposed butter and sugar from the ramekins. Place ramekins on a baking sheet and bake about 12 minutes, until puffed. Serve hot with whipped cream if desired.

CHOCOLATE FONDANT

ONE IF BY LAND, TWO IF BY SEA

Acknowledged to be one of the most romantic dining rooms in
Manhattan, One If by Land, TIBS, as it is known, is tucked into a flower-filled,
candlelit landmark carriage house—it was once owned by Aaron Burr—
on a quiet Greenwich Village street. It even has a working fireplace. And it
remains one of the few bastions of Continental cooking, offering elaborate
special-occasion standbys like oysters, foie gras, smoked salmon, beef
Wellington, and rack of lamb. And for dessert, there is plenty of chocolate:
a soufflé, a tart, and these individual molten chocolate cakes, served warm.

9 ounces (18 tablespoons; 2 sticks plus 2 tablespoons) unsalted butter

3 tablespoons unsweetened cocoa

6 ounces bittersweet chocolate, at least 70% cacao solids (see tip)

½ vanilla bean, halved lengthwise, seeds scraped out and reserved

6 eggs, separated, at room temperature

⅓ cup sugar

1 tablespoon all-purpose flour

Vanilla ice cream or whipped cream, for serving

Many of the finer brands of semisweet and bittersweet chocolate are now sold with the percentage of cacao solids indicated on the label. The higher the percentage, the more bitter the chocolate.

Use 2 tablespoons of the butter to grease 8 (4-ounce) soufflé dishes or ramekins. Muffin tins can be used. Dust the ramekins with the cocoa.

Place the remaining 2 sticks of butter, the chocolate, and vanilla seeds in the top of a double boiler and stir over simmering water until the mixture is melted and smooth. Transfer to a large mixing bowl and set aside to cool.

Beat the egg whites until frothy, then beat until softly peaked, adding the sugar gradually. Fold the flour into the chocolate mixture. Lightly beat the egg yolks, then stir them into the chocolate mixture. Fold in the egg whites. Transfer the mixture to the prepared ramekins, cover with plastic wrap, and refrigerate overnight.

About 30 minutes before serving time, preheat the oven to 350 degrees. Place the ramekins in the oven and bake about 12 minutes. The tops of the cakes will be barely firm but the cakes will show signs of releasing around the sides. A cake tester will not come out clean. Remove the cakes from the oven, quickly run a knife around each, then invert them onto individual plates. If you have used muffin tins, place a baking sheet or a plastic cutting board over the tins to invert them all at once. Serve the cakes before they cool and start to sink, with whipped cream or ice cream alongside.

10-year-old Malmsey Madeira, another Madeira, or a red dessert wine

MEXICAN ALMOND TART

MAYA

Richard Sandoval has a far-flung restaurant empire that touches down in New York and Dubai, with stops in Colorado, San Francisco, Las Vegas, and Mexico in between. His is refined Mexican cuisine, high-end and deeply flavorful, as demonstrated by this unusual tart that depends on fresh corn and sweetened condensed milk for its richness.

SERVES 8 TO 10

1¼ cups almond flour
½ cup all-purpose flour
½ teaspoon salt
½ cup (1 stick) soft unsalted butter
¼ cup sugar
2 large egg yolks
1 cup fresh corn kernels
2 large whole eggs
7 ounces sweetened condensed milk
½ cup whole milk
1 packet unflavored gelatin
¼ cup dark rum
1 teaspoon almond extract
¾ cup heavy cream
2 tablespoons chopped toasted almonds

🍷 A sweet dessert wine, like a forti-
fied orange Muscat from California

 Almond flour can be found in fancy food shops, and online. You can grind your own almonds in a food processor, but the result will not be as fine.

Whisk the flours and the salt together in a bowl. Set aside.

In an electric mixer, cream the butter and sugar until light and beat in the egg yolks one at a time. Stir in the dry ingredients until the mixture becomes a soft dough. Form it into a flat disk, wrap in plastic, and refrigerate for 30 minutes.

Preheat the oven to 325 degrees. Press the dough into the bottom and up the sides of a 8-inch tart pan with a removable bottom and bake until lightly browned, about 20 minutes. Cool.

Place the corn kernels, whole eggs, condensed milk, and whole milk in a blender. Puree. Strain the mixture. Place it in a heavy saucepan and cook it gently, stirring with a wooden spoon, until the mixture thickens and forms a custard sauce that coats the back of the spoon. Do not overcook or the eggs will curdle. Alternatively, the mixture can be cooked in the top of a double boiler.

Soften the gelatin in ¼ cup water and whisk it into the warm custard. Add the rum and the almond extract. Allow it to cool to room temperature, then cover and refrigerate it until it is chilled and has set. Remove the custard from the refrigerator and whisk to soften and blend it. Whip the heavy cream until softly peaked. Fold it into the rum and corn custard.

Spoon the mixture into the tart shell. Scatter the almonds near the edge and refrigerate until ready to serve.

APPLE AND WALNUT CRUMBLE

BRAEBURN

Brian Bistrong has followed the dream of many a chef. He opened his own modest yet warm and welcoming restaurant in Greenwich Village. His food has always been market-driven and seasonal, and at Braeburn it is more so than ever. This dessert capitalizes on the sweetness of the Braeburn apple that gave the restaurant its name and adds spice and crunch at the same time. The hominess of the dish demonstrates the chef's approach to cooking.

SERVES 6

6½ tablespoons soft unsalted butter

2 cups coarsely chopped walnuts

½ teaspoon cornstarch

4 teaspoons lemon juice

4 cups peeled, cored, diced Granny Smith apples (about 3 apples)

4 cups peeled, cored, diced Braeburn or other sweet, crisp apples (about 3 apples)

1 cup granulated sugar

Salt

¼ teaspoon cinnamon

¼ teaspoon ground nutmeg

1 cup flour

¼ cup packed light brown sugar

1 teaspoon vanilla extract

Vanilla ice cream, for serving

By baking the topping separately from the fruit at first, the flavors and textures retain their character. The crumble can be completely assembled in advance, and the final baking can be done shortly before the dessert is to be served.

Preheat the oven to 350 degrees. Grease an 8-inch round baking dish with ½ tablespoon of the butter. While the oven is heating, spread the nuts on a baking sheet and lightly toast them, about 5 minutes. Remove from the oven.

Whisk the cornstarch and the lemon juice together in a large bowl until the cornstarch is dissolved. Add the toasted walnuts, the apples, ⅔ cup of the granulated sugar, a pinch of salt, the cinnamon, and nutmeg and mix to combine. Spread in the baking dish, cover and bake about 30 minutes, until the apples are tender.

In a food processor combine the flour, ¼ cup of the remaining granulated sugar, the brown sugar, a pinch of salt, and the vanilla. Pulse briefly to combine. Add the butter in pieces and pulse until the mixture clumps, 15 to 20 seconds. Spread on a baking sheet and bake until crisp but not browned, about 20 minutes.

When the apples are done, remove the baking dish from the oven. Stir the mixture. Scatter the crumble topping over the fruit and sprinkle with the remaining granulated sugar. Bake until browned and bubbly, about 30 minutes. Serve with ice cream.

CHERRY CLAFOUTI

Clinton Street on the Lower East Side is now a bona fide Restaurant Row. Its fine, mostly small places signal the changes in this once-Jewish area that now caters to the young and trendy. Wylie Dufresne, who worked with Jean-Georges Vongerichten, first made his mark cooking inventive American fare in a closet-size kitchen at 71 Clinton Fresh Food. He then moved across the street and opened wd50, a combination of his initials and the street address. Now his creativity is working overtime, layering anchovies on blocks of foie gras, and cutting thread-like "noodles" out of squid. Sam Mason, the pastry chef, is no slouch when it comes to invention, either. His clafouti, a kind of French batter cake, is baked in a pastry shell and relies on a filling of cherries marinated with pepper and star anise.

SERVES 6 TO 8

1½ cups granulated sugar

1 cup ruby port

6 whole black peppercorns

1 piece star anise

Zest of 1 orange, grated

1 vanilla bean, halved lengthwise, seeds scraped out and reserved

1 pound cherries, pitted

¾ cup sliced almonds

1½ tablespoons plus 2 cups all-purpose flour, and more for work surface

1 cup heavy cream

3 whole eggs

3 egg yolks

9 tablespoons soft unsalted butter

½ cup sifted confectioners' sugar

½ teaspoon salt

1 tablespoon lightly toasted chopped, unsalted pistachios

Combine 1 cup of the granulated sugar with ¼ cup water in a heavy saucepan. Cook over high heat, watching carefully, until the mixture just begins to color. Stir in 1 cup very hot water and mix until the sugar has dissolved. Add the port, peppercorns, star anise, orange zest, vanilla bean with seeds, and cherries. Simmer for 10 minutes. Remove from the heat, allow to cool to room temperature, cover, and refrigerate overnight.

While the cherries are cooking, place the almonds in a dry skillet and toast. Grind very fine in a blender. Mix the ground almonds with the 1½ tablespoons flour and the remaining ½ cup of granulated sugar. Bring the cream to a boil. In a bowl, beat 2 of the whole eggs with the 3 egg yolks, and gradually beat in the cream. Whisk in the almond mixture. Cover and refrigerate overnight.

Also on the day before you bake the clafouti, make the pastry. Beat the butter with the confectioners' sugar. Slowly beat in the remaining egg. Mix the remaining 2 cups of flour with the salt and stir into the butter mixture. Beat for a minute or so to make a tender dough. Wrap in plastic and refrigerate.

 Refrigerating the batter overnight allows the flavor of the almonds to intensify.

Start to assemble the clafouti about an hour before it is to be served. Preheat the oven to 425 degrees. Allow the dough to come nearly to room temperature, then roll it on a lightly floured surface and fit it into a 10-inch tart pan. Prick the surface, line it with foil, weight it with pastry weights, and bake about 10 minutes. Remove it from the oven and reduce the temperature to 350 degrees.

Drain the cherries well, discarding the whole spices and reserving the syrup. Spread the cherries on the partially-baked pastry. Whisk the almond mixture and pour it over the cherries. Place the tart pan in the oven and bake about 35 minutes, until just set. Remove from the oven. Scatter the pistachios on top and drizzle with a little of the syrup.

Coteaux du Layon or a vintage port

Serve while still warm, with more of the syrup alongside.

RASPBERRY CROSTADA

> *Eli Zabar has been in the restaurant business* about as long as he has had food markets on the Upper East Side. The café at E.A.T. on Madison Avenue feeds a well-heeled clientele looking for a place to eat near the Metropolitan Museum of Art. The upstairs café at the Vinegar Factory, on the same Yorkville block as his bread bakery, has long been a venue for brunch and parties. Taste is the most ambitious of his restaurants, a café by day and a more serious place with a wine bar in the evening. Scott Bieber, the chef, takes advantage of all the fine ingredients that come into the market. His lemon meringue cake is a signature, but these jam-filled raspberry tartlets are easier to manage at home.

SERVES 12

3 cups all-purpose flour, plus additional for kneading and rolling

½ teaspoon salt

¾ cup granulated sugar

1½ cups (3 sticks) cold unsalted butter, diced

3 egg yolks

1 whole egg

1½ cups good raspberry jam (see tip)

1½ pints fresh raspberries

Sifted confectioners' sugar

Whipped cream or vanilla ice cream, optional

Place the flour, salt, and granulated sugar in a food processor. Pulse briefly to mix. Add the butter and pulse just until the mixture is crumbly. Lightly beat 2 of the egg yolks and the whole egg together. Add them to the food processor, then pulse until a dough starts to form. If the mixture is too dry to gather into a ball, sprinkle with a little cold water and pulse again. Briefly knead the dough, flatten it into a disk, wrap it in plastic, and refrigerate it at least an hour.

Roll out the dough to a thickness of ⅛ inch on a floured surface. Cut as many 5-inch-diameter circles as you can. This first pass should yield about 9 circles. Reroll your scraps and you'll be able to cut out 3 more.

Cover a large baking sheet with parchment.

Spread 2 tablespoons of the jam in the center of each pastry circle, leaving a ½-inch border. Fold the border over, pleating it as you go, so each crostada has a pastry border and a jam center. Beat the remaining egg yolk with a tablespoon of water and brush this wash on the pastry edges.

Try to use seedless raspberry jam in the filling. Other fruits—fresh blueberries and blueberry jam, strawberries and strawberry jam, and even fig—would work well, too.

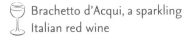 Brachetto d'Acqui, a sparkling Italian red wine

With a wide, flat spatula, arrange the crostadas on the baking sheet and refrigerate 15 minutes. Preheat the oven to 400 degrees. Place the crostadas in the oven and bake until they're golden, about 25 minutes. Transfer the pastries from the pan to a rack to cool. Arrange fresh raspberries over the jam, standing them closely at attention. Dust with confectioners' sugar and serve. Whipped cream or vanilla ice cream alongside? Why not!

HONEY PANNA COTTA

Having made his mark on the Smith Street restaurant row in Boerum Hill, Brooklyn, Adam Shepard and his partners opened a larger version of Lunetta in Manhattan, in the Flatiron district. Yet Brooklyn is where the soul of this restaurant resides. It is there that the lush ricotta is made in house. At both locations the ricotta is served as an appetizer, spread on toasted country bread with a drizzle of honey. This dessert, a honeyed, creamy panna cotta, is clearly on the same wavelength as the appetizer. Interpretive Italian is in very good hands in both restaurants.

SERVES 8

5 cups heavy cream

3 vanilla beans, split lengthwise

1½ cups floral honey

1½ packets (4 teaspoons) unflavored gelatin

The panna cottas, like the typical ceramic ramekins, are very white. A colorful garnish for each, like a small strip of candied orange peel, or a few golden raisins plumped in a little warm rum and drained, would be a nice touch.

Combine the heavy cream, vanilla beans, and 1 cup of the honey in a saucepan. Simmer until warm and combined.

Soften the gelatin in ¼ cup water in a metal measuring cup. Place the cup in a pan with a little water in it and heat until the gelatin liquefies. Whisk the gelatin into the warm cream and bring to a simmer. Remove from the heat. Place the saucepan in a big bowl of ice and water to cool it down. When cool, remove the vanilla beans.

Mix the remaining honey with 2 tablespoons water. Spoon this mixture into the bottom of eight 6-ounce ramekins. Pour in the cooled cream mixture. Cover the ramekins with plastic wrap and refrigerate until cold and set, about 12 hours.

Serve in the ramekins.

A smooth Müller-Thurgau from Italy, a low-acid, medium-sweet wine with Muscat hints, pairs well with desserts

LEMON FIG TART

Veritas is as much about wine as it is about food. This small, but graciously elegant spot in the Flatiron district has a deep cellar, with some of the best Rhône Valley and California bottles. Like the room, the food is finely crafted. Both are more subtle than splashy, and both rely on the best materials at hand. This lemon dessert is a complex affair, but one that should not daunt an experienced home cook.

SERVES 8 TO 12

7½ tablespoons soft unsalted butter

5 tablespoons granulated sugar

½ teaspoon salt

3 vanilla beans, split lengthwise

½ cup cake flour

1¼ cups toasted almonds, finely chopped

½ cup almond flour

¼ cup confectioners' sugar

2 tablespoons all-purpose flour

2 large egg whites, at room temperature

½ cup heavy cream

14 ounces white chocolate

6 tablespoons lemon juice

1 tablespoon corn syrup

4 fresh black figs, quartered

Preheat the oven to 375 degrees. Cream 5 tablespoons of the butter with 2 tablespoons of the granulated sugar. Add the salt and the seeds from 1 vanilla bean. Fold in the cake flour and the chopped almonds to form a dough. Press the dough into the bottom of a 9-inch springform pan. Bake until golden, about 20 minutes. Allow to cool.

Reduce the oven heat to 300 degrees. Use ½ tablespoon of the butter to grease a 9-inch cake pan. In a small bowl whisk together the almond flour, confectioners' sugar, and all-purpose flour. Whip the egg whites with the remaining 3 tablespoons of the sugar until stiff. Fold in the flour mixture. Fold in 2 tablespoons of the cream. Scrape out the seeds from the remaining 2 vanilla beans into the mixture. Spread the batter in the pan and bake until lightly golden and springy to the touch. Allow to cool.

Break up the white chocolate and place it in a bowl. Combine the lemon juice, remaining cream, and corn syrup in a small saucepan and heat barely to a simmer. Pour over the chocolate. Stir until the chocolate has melted. Stir in the remaining 2 tablespoons of the butter.

The best part of the vanilla bean is the seeds that can be scraped out from the center. But do not discard the pods that remain—they are too expensive to waste. Place them in a canister of granulated sugar and, before you know it, you will have vanilla sugar.

Spread a thin film of the lemon and white chocolate mixture on the almond crust. Unmold the vanilla sponge and place it over the crust. Pour in the rest of the lemon-white chocolate mixture. Refrigerate at least 4 hours. Remove the sides of the pan. Decorate the top of the dessert with quartered figs. Serve.

ANDRÉ SOLTNER'S CHOCOLATE MOUSSE
T-BAR STEAK AND LOUNGE

Lutèce, Chef André Soltner's townhouse French restaurant, is no more. The premises are empty, and the question remains whether anyone will ever take it over and reopen it. In the meantime, Soltner teaches at the French Culinary Institute in SoHo, and his recipe for chocolate mousse lives on at T-Bar Steak & Lounge on the Upper East Side. The owner of the restaurant, Tony Fortuna, one of New York's most genial hosts, decided to pay homage to his friend Soltner by putting this dessert on the menu.

3 large eggs

1 cup sugar

1⅔ cups heavy cream, plus additional to make whipped cream garnish if desired

2 tablespoons dark rum

5 ounces semisweet chocolate (about 66%), melted and cooled

2 tablespoons unsalted butter, melted and cooled

1 tablespoon vanilla extract or espresso

Place the whites from 2 of the eggs in the bowl of an electric mixer. Start to whip them on low speed. Place ½ cup of the sugar and 2 tablespoons water in a small saucepan and boil until the mixture registers 239 degrees on a candy thermometer. When the egg whites form soft peaks, slowly drizzle in the sugar syrup, whipping on high speed for several minutes until the mixture is stiff and glossy. Set aside.

In a saucepan, lightly beat the remaining whole egg and 2 egg yolks with ⅔ cup of the cream, the rum, and remaining ½ cup of sugar. Place over medium heat and cook, stirring, until the mixture thickens enough to coat the back of a wooden spoon. Remove the custard from the heat and stir in the melted chocolate. Allow to cool, or chill it in a metal bowl set in a larger bowl of ice water.

When the custard has cooled, beat the remaining cream until softly peaked. Fold in the egg white mixture, then fold in the chocolate custard. Fold in the butter and vanilla or espresso.

Spoon the mixture into goblets or ramekins, or into a handsome bowl, and chill overnight before serving. Additional whipped cream is an optional embellishment.

 Port or Hungarian tokay would have enough sweetness to complement the chocolate mousse.

ILONA TORTE

CAFÉ DES ARTISTES

> *With its splendid Howard Chandle Christy paintings* and warm, clubby atmosphere, Café des Artistes has long been a magnet for New Yorkers and tourists alike. And its location, a block or so from Lincoln Center, has made it something of a hangout for musicians. That's also because its co-owner, George Lang, is a violinist and a close friend of a number of the soloists and conductors on the New York concert scene. The food is Continental with hints of Middle Europe, thanks to Lang, a Hungarian émigré who also owns restaurants in Budapest. The restaurant's name comes from its location, in a building called the Hotel des Artistes, on a block where most of the buildings were constructed with duplexes and double-height windows for artists' studios. The Ilona Torte is a Hungarian confection that Lang named for his mother and for one of his daughters.

SERVES 12

Butter and all-purpose flour for pan

13 ounces semisweet chocolate, coarsely chopped

1 cup granulated sugar

26 tablespoons (3 sticks plus 2 tablespoons) soft unsalted butter

8 eggs, separated, at room temperature

8 ounces walnuts, ground (about 1¼ cups)

2 tablespoons soft white bread crumbs

Pinch of salt

3 tablespoons instant espresso powder

3 egg yolks

1 cup confectioners' sugar, sifted

2 tablespoons chopped walnuts

Preheat the oven to 375 degrees. Butter a 10-inch springform pan. Line the bottom with parchment. Dust the pan with flour, shaking out any excess.

Place 5 ounces of the chocolate, the granulated sugar, and ¼ cup water in a metal bowl set over a pan of simmering water. Heat, stirring, until the chocolate melts and the sugar dissolves, 5 to 6 minutes. Set aside.

In an electric mixer, beat 6 tablespoons of the soft butter until light. Beat in the 8 egg yolks one at a time until smooth and creamy. On low speed beat in the chocolate mixture, then the ground walnuts and bread crumbs.

In a separate bowl beat the 8 egg whites with salt and 1 tablespoon of ice water until stiffly peaked but still creamy. Fold the whites into the chocolate mixture. Because the chocolate mixture is quite heavy, it will be slow going at first. When it's well-blended, spoon the batter into the pan, smooth the top, and bake about 40 minutes, until the top is firm to the touch and a cake tester comes out clean. Place the cake on a rack and allow it to cool in the pan.

In order to make handling easier, when you split the cake to fill and frost it, be sure that the cut sides are what will be covered with the filling and that the smooth sides form the bottom and top of the cake.

The cake will sink; not to worry.

When cake is cool, place remaining 8 ounces of chocolate with the espresso powder and ½ cup boiling water in a metal bowl over simmering water. Stir to make a smooth mixture. Remove from heat and beat in the 3 egg yolks, one at a time.

In an electric mixer beat the remaining 20 tablespoons of soft butter until creamy. Gradually beat in the confectioners' sugar, mixing well. Stir in the chocolate mixture.

When cake has cooled completely, remove it from the pan, invert it, and peel off the parchment. Use a large serrated knife to slice the torte horizontally into 2 layers. Place the top half cut side up on a platter. Frost it with 1 cup of the buttercream. Place the second layer cut side down on top. Frost top and sides with remaining buttercream. Sprinkle chopped walnuts on top and serve.

A fine, sweet Tokay

RAVANI, ALMOND CAKE WITH CITRUS SYRUP

MOLYVOS

A rustic home of regional Greek cooking in Midtown, Molyvos is decorated with copperware, pottery, and family photos from the owners, the Livanos family, who own several restaurants in Westchester County as well as Oceana, a fine seafood establishment, in Manhattan. Molyvos is the place for traditional Greek dining, from the array of *meze* appetizers to the syrupy desserts. The wine list, too, offers a rich assortment of wines from the Greek mainland and the islands, which can be expertly paired with the food.

13 tablespoons (1 stick plus 5 tablespoons) soft unsalted butter

⅓ cup unblanched almonds, finely
chopped

¾ cup all-purpose flour

1½ cups semolina flour

1½ teaspoons baking powder

1 teaspoon baking soda

4 eggs, separated, at room
temperature

1 teaspoon vanilla extract

1½ cups sugar

Pinch salt

1 cup honey

2 teaspoons grated orange zest

2 cups whole-milk yogurt,
preferably Greek, for serving

1 orange, cut in segments,
pith removed, for serving

> When pouring the hot syrup over the cake, do it very gradually. Allow the syrup to be absorbed before adding more, so it will penetrate evenly.

Preheat the oven to 325 degrees. Use 1 tablespoon of the butter to grease a 6-cup loaf pan. Line the bottom with parchment paper and butter the paper.

Place the almonds, all-purpose flour, semolina flour, baking powder, and baking soda in a bowl and whisk together to combine.

Using an electric mixer on medium-high speed, beat the egg yolks, vanilla, and ¾ cup of the sugar until very thick and light. Gradually beat in remaining 12 tablespoons butter, beating until creamy. In a separate mixing bowl, beat the egg whites at medium-high speed with salt until they hold firm peaks but are still creamy.

Return the egg yolk bowl to the mixer and on low speed gradually beat in the dry ingredients. The mixture will be stiff. By hand, stir one-fourth of the beaten egg whites into the batter, then fold in the rest. Spoon the batter into the pan and smooth the top. Bake until golden and cake tester comes out clean, about 50 minutes. Remove cake from oven and place the pan on a rack to cool.

Place remaining ¾ cup of sugar with the honey, orange zest, and 3 cups water in a saucepan. Bring to a boil and simmer 5 minutes. Remove from heat. Using a thin bamboo skewer, poke down into the cake over the entire surface. Gradually pour two-thirds of the hot syrup over cake. Allow to stand at least 2 hours.

Remove the cake from the pan and slice. Serve topped with yogurt and orange segments, with remaining citrus syrup spooned over.

 Moscato of Limnos, or other sweet moscato wine

DRINKS

FARMER'S LEMONADE

Maury Rubin's City Bakery began as a café a few steps from the Union Square Greenmarket. It has since moved to larger quarters about a block away. Now, in addition to an expanded array of fresh baked goods, it has assorted food buffets for breakfast, lunch, and dinner; a soda fountain that serves homemade ice cream and root beer floats; and a "chocolate room," an alcove lined with chocolate confections. Rubin also throws "block parties" in his restaurant to celebrate the harvest.

SERVES 6

Juice of 15 large lemons
½ cup sugar
½ cup heavy cream

When mixing in the sugar and water, it helps to use your hands to rub the sugar so it will dissolve faster.

Place the lemon juice in a large bowl or 2-quart pitcher. Whisk in the sugar and add 4 cups cold water. Whisk until the sugar has dissolved. Whisk in the heavy cream. Pour over ice and serve.

ROSSINI COCKTAIL

HARRY CIPRIANI

There is no Harry's Bar in New York, but nonetheless there is a major Cipriani presence. Harry Cipriani, the first of the collection to open, remains the flagship. It has a menu that is a close copy of the original in Venice, with carpaccio, risottos, simple pastas, fish and meat, and sumptuous desserts. The furnishings are lower than normal, another signature of the Cipriani style. The SoHo restaurant called Downtown, Cipriani Dolci in Grand Central Terminal, the Rainbow Room and Rainbow Grill, and Cipriani 42nd Street, a vast catering hall in the former Bowery Saving Bank building, constitute the rest of the Cipriani group. Their signature drink is the Bellini, a combination of fresh white peach puree and sparkling prosecco created by Arrigo Cipriani in Venice. But everyone serves Bellinis these days. The Rossini is a variation, made only when good fresh strawberries are available.

SERVES 4

1 pint fresh strawberries
2 teaspoons sugar, or to taste
1 bottle prosecco, chilled

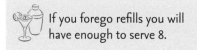 If you forego refills you will have enough to serve 8.

Trim the strawberries, reserving 4 nice ones for garnish. Puree the rest in a blender until very smooth. If the puree is very tart, sweeten it lightly with the sugar—it should not be very sweet. Chill the puree.

To serve, spoon about 1½ tablespoons of the puree into each of 4 Champagne flutes. Slowly pour in the prosecco. Garnish each drink with a strawberry perched on the rim of the glass. You should have enough of the puree and wine for a second round of drinks.

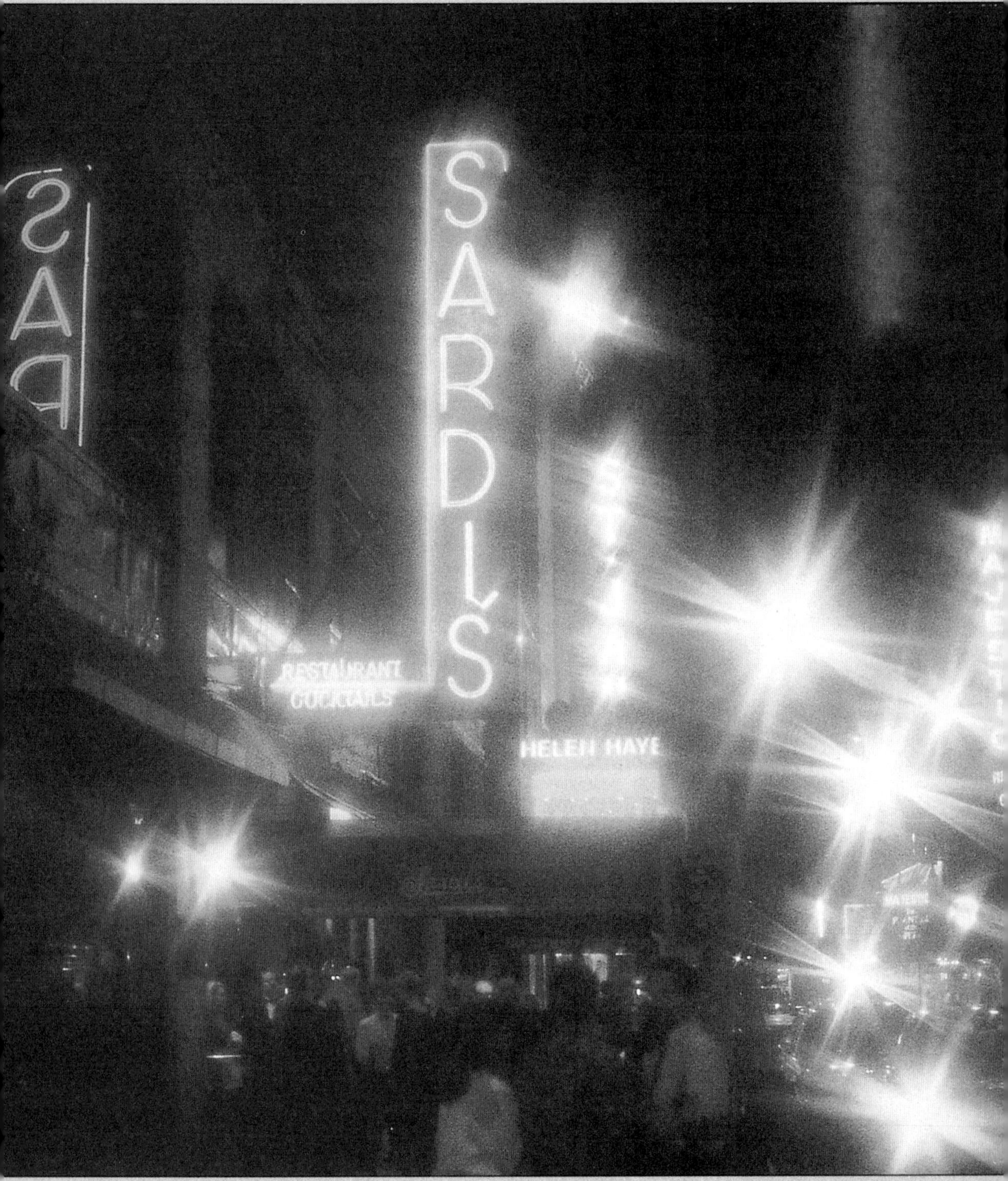
SARDI'S
RESTAURANT
HELEN HAYE

COSMOPOLITAN

SARDI'S

Sardi's remains the place of choice for pre- and post-theater drinks, dining, and celebrations, as it has been since Vincent Sardi opened it in 1921. The stars are immortalized in caricatures that cover the walls of the restaurant. Sardi's is famous for its opening night parties, often held on the restaurant's second floor, removed from the public dining room, so the first reviews can be read to cheers or tears. Rather than actually dining on the restaurant's famous lasagna or cannelloni on these occasions, most Broadway denizens just prefer a drink.

SERVES 2

½ ounce dry vermouth
2½ ounces Cointreau
6 ounces vodka
½ cup cranberry juice
Juice of ½ lime

Combine the vermouth, Cointreau, vodka, and cranberry juice with ice cubes in a cocktail shaker. Shake to blend. Add the lime juice, stir, and strain into chilled martini glasses.

MOJITO

CALLE OCHO

In recent years, Latin food has given a hot new beat to New York dining, and put mint-infused mojitos on the drink list. Caribbean and South American cooking was always a presence in neighborhoods in the Bronx and Queens and on the Upper West Side, but it has now become a mainstream cuisine. Calle Ocho, named for the Cuban boulevard in Miami, is an Upper West Side example of this new wave, in a part of the city where bodegas and diners that offer Cuban-Criolla rice and beans still survive, untouched by trends. Calle Ocho is part of an eclectic restaurant collection that includes Bar Bao for Vietnamese food.

SERVES 4

1 bunch mint

¼ cup fresh lime juice

4 ounces light rum

1 lime, cut in 4 wedges

3 cups ice cubes

2½ cups sparkling water or club soda, approximately

This mojito is made without sugar, but for a slightly sweeter drink, a tablespoon of simple syrup can be stirred in with the lime and mint. Make the simple syrup by simmering 2 parts sugar to 1 of water until the sugar dissolves, then cool.

If you have a nice large cocktail shaker, now is the time to take it out. Place half the mint in it, add the lime juice, and bruise the mint with a muddler or wooden spoon. Add the rum.

Divide the remaining mint among 4 large old-fashioned glasses, lightly squeeze in the lime wedges, and drop them in. Add about ½ cup of ice to each of the glasses. Add the remaining ice to the cocktail shaker and shake well. Strain the mixture into the glasses, fill each with sparkling water, and serve.

CEREAL MILK

Back in August of 2004, an unknown chef, David Chang, along with his partner Joaquin Baca, opened an unadorned and frankly uncomfortable but cheap noodle bar in the East Village. Called Momofuku (which means lucky peach in Japanese), this small spot hardly seemed poised to become a stunning phenomenon. But it did, and Chang would become a superstar chef. One clue to its oncoming success, perhaps, was the line of people outside waiting for seats at the counter so they could scarf down bowls of ramen with Berkshire pork. Three years later, Momofuku Ssäm Bar, with tables, not just a counter, followed. Soon after, Momofuku Noodle Bar moved to larger digs a block away and the original space was turned into Ko, serving pricey tasting menus for lunch and dinner. The most recent addition to this chainlet is Momofuku Bakery and Milk Bar , where Christina Tosi, the pastry chef, confers with Chang to come up with some wild fantasies, like chorizo challah, salty caramel-pistachio soft-serve ice cream, and candy bar pie. A list of flavored organic milks includes cereal milk, an infusion of baked corn flakes with a touch of brown sugar and salt.

3 cups Kellogg's corn flakes or
　organic corn flakes

2¾ cups whole milk, preferably
　organic

⅛ teaspoon salt

1½ to 2 tablespoons light brown
　sugar

> Just before serving, some soft-serve or softened regular ice cream can be blended in to make a milk shake. At Momofuku, they like it with their snickerdoodle soft-serve, but vanilla, chocolate, coffee, or banana are also good.

Preheat the oven to 275 degrees. Spread the corn flakes on a baking sheet and bake for 20 minutes. Remove them and allow them to cool. Place the corn flakes in a 1-quart plastic container that has a lid. Add the milk, give it a shake, cover, and set it aside for 30 minutes.

Strain the milk into a bowl through a chinois or a very fine strainer. You can gently press down on the corn flakes once, but no more. Stir the corn flakes and allow the milk to drip through.

Add the salt and 1½ tablespoons of the brown sugar to the milk. Use a handheld blender or electric mixer to blend just until the sugar and salt have dissolved and the milk turns frothy. Add more sugar if desired and blend again. Chill. Blend again to froth the mixture just before serving.

WINE IN NEW YORK RESTAURANTS

New York is, unquestionably, the wine capital of the world. With access to more wine at every level of quality and price than any other city—10,000 labels, in fact—New Yorkers can pick and choose wines from some of the most sophisticated lists in the world. Wines of every conceivable variety can be found from virtually every country, and almost every producer.

Nearly 20,000 restaurants spread across five boroughs present wine lists that mirror the New York population—diverse and staggering—ranging from a single selection "house pour" wine to exhaustive inventories boasting more than 4,000 selections. The lists offer wines from the city's backyard, the Hudson Valley and Long Island, and from such far-flung regions as New Zealand, South Africa, Chile, and Croatia.

This is a development of fairly recent vintage, just in the past twenty-five years. My own personal collection of wine lists includes one from the '21' Club dating from 1959. It is long, seventy pages. The first fifty list French wines only, primarily from Bordeaux and Burgundy. These are followed by fifteen pages of German wines, leaving the last five for a sparse inventory of Italian, Spanish, and California wines. In those days, when the cocktail was more important than wine, a list like that was the exception.

When Windows on the World opened on top of One World Trade Center in 1976, the owner, Joe Baum, instructed me to "create the best wine list that New York has ever seen." Windows immediately became known as having one of the finest wine lists in the country, one that was a pioneer in recognizing what California had to offer. It also ended up with the highest wine sales for any restaurant in the world. Another benefit of the great wine list was that it attracted many wine enthusiasts to the restaurant and to the downtown area.

The same year that Windows opened, The Four Seasons, another of Joe Baum's inspirations, held its first California barrel tasting dinner. It featured the 1975 vintage of eighteen wineries, as yet unbottled, all the wines paired with a gala menu. The event was meant as a promotion for the wines, not for the restaurant, but it served both purposes. The annual tradition lasted for ten years, by which time New York had become a solid wine-drinking city and The Four Seasons had become one of the best-known venues for wines and wine dinners.

Today, New York's savvy restaurateurs and their clients know that a great restaurant is in no small part defined by the quality of its wine list. That fine wines and good food are at the heart of a memorable meal seems obvious. The wine director and the wine list are decisive in defining whether a restaurant is merely good or truly great. Diners judge restaurants as much by their wine lists as by their menus, service, and decor. Many restaurateurs report that more than 40% of their revenue is from wine sales, and some of them wisely use their wine list as a promotional vehicle.

New York restaurateurs such as Danny Meyer not only have great wine lists but wine service to match. Three of his restaurants have won the James Beard Award for outstanding wine service: Union Square Cafe (1999), Gramercy Tavern (2002), and Eleven Madison Park (2008). Other winners include Chanterelle (1996) under the direction of Roger Dagorn, who has been the super sommelier of New York City for the last seventeen years. Daniel (2003) has hired wine personality Daniel Johnnes, winner of the James Beard Outstanding Wine & Spirits Professional Award in 2006, to run all of Daniel Boulud's Dinex restaurant group wine programs. Author, restaurateur, and wine importer Joe Bastianich has created top Italian wine lists at Babbo and Del Posto.

Restaurant guru Drew Nieporent, owner of such restaurants as Tribeca Grill and Nobu, named his first restaurant after a vineyard in Burgundy, Montrachet. In 2008 he reopened the same spot with a new menu, wine list, and another name taken from a Burgundy vineyard, Corton.

Alan Stillman, owner of Smith & Wollensky New York, has cleverly used wine to help promote his restaurants by creating a twice-a-year Wine Week, during which customers are treated with an array of wines freely poured at any of his restaurants during lunch. Smith & Wollensky also boasts one of this country's largest lists of American wines (more than eight hundred). At one of his other restaurants, Maloney & Porcelli, diners can indulge themselves with a three-course menu including four wines for a special price every Friday, Saturday, and Sunday evening.

Most of the wine-friendly restaurants in New York City have a sommelier or wine director. At Veritas always ask to discuss your selection with Tim Kopec. The same can be said for Phil Pratt ('21' Club), Eric Zillier (Alto), Renzo Rapacioli (Barolo), and Bernie Sun (Jean Georges). At Le Bernardin, chief sommelier Aldo Sohm has won the title of the Best Sommelier in the World for 2008. Behind-the-scenes wine director Laura Maniec of B.R. Guest restaurant group maintains wine lists and wine service in all their restaurants, such as Fiamma. Master sommelier Fred Dexheimer does the same for all of the BLT restaurants.

Some of the classic French and Italian restaurants such as Adour Alain Ducasse, Bouley, Le Cirque, Felidia, Barbetta, and I Trulli have created great wine cellars to go along with their excellent cuisine. One of the largest wine lists in New York City can be found at Cru. Actually it is two wine lists (one for white, one for red)—with more than 4,200 choices selected by Robert Bohr.

New Yorkers take their Chinese food seriously, so don't be surprised when you are presented a wine list at one of the great Chinese restaurants. Not in Chinatown, mind you, but in uptown places like Chin Chin. To pair with the newly popular tapas, restaurants offer sherries and deep collections of fine Spanish wines. And now sake lists are showing up, and not only in Japanese restaurants.

One of the pioneers of great wines at great prices is back. Harry Poulakakos has reopened Harry's Café and Steak in the financial district, and the restaurant offers an extensive selection of value wines with more than one hundred under fifty dollars.

And it is not just a Manhattan phenomenon. Across the Brooklyn Bridge there are others. At the River Café, wine director Joe DeLissio has a superb list. In fact, these days it is hard to find a good restaurant that does not have a solid selection of wines, designed to complement the food, in a range of prices. And, this being New York, order a pepperoni pizza somewhere and it would not be surprising to be handed a wine list so you can choose a nice bottle of red to go with it!

DESIGN IN NEW YORK RESTAURANTS

DAVID ROCKWELL

When the Russian impresario Sergei Diaghilev wanted Jean Cocteau to create a libretto for his dance company, he presented the 23-year-old Parisian literary sensation with the two-word artistic challenge: "Astonish me."

The same demand inevitably punctuates the conversation whenever a member of New York City's intrepid band of restaurateurs approaches a designer with the idea for a potential project. Restaurateurs function in a supercharged, highly competitive, make-or-break atmosphere, and their lust for astonishment reflects the fact that restaurant openings have become as significant a cultural and social event as the premiere of the latest Broadway extravaganza.

It is no surprise then that the restaurant community replicates the rituals commonly associated with the theater. In common with a Broadway production, a new restaurant goes out of its way to generate anticipatory publicity. As the opening approaches, the restaurant stages a series of dress rehearsals with friends cast in the roles of patrons. A demanding assortment of critics, fellow restaurateurs, opinion makers, and food savvy patrons fills the tables as soon as the curtain officially rings up. Immediately afterwards, they unhesitatingly deliver public proclamations revealing how much astonishment they experienced—or didn't.

In this context, it is no wonder that a restaurateur must function as choreographer, director, and conductor all in one, producing the dining experience as if it were a three-act play. Yet the marriage of dining and showmanship is not new: It has been with us since March 1830, when the Swiss-born brothers, John and Peter Delmonico, expanded their confectionery shop into New York's first restaurant. After the brothers instituted their introductory menu, they went on to compile a list of 340 entrées, stock their cellar with 16,000 bottles of the best French wine, and in 1861, hire the first celebrity chef, Charles Ranhofer. Show business obviously coursed through the brothers' bloodstreams.

In 1968, at the age of 11, I dined with two of my older brothers at our first New York restaurant, a branch of the now-legendary Schrafft's chain. Although we were boisterous youths, the refined atmosphere so overwhelmed us that we automatically sat up straight and dropped our voices to whispers. Schrafft's served moderately priced food, and when our waitress (who wore a pastel handkerchief in her hair!) served my cheeseburger and fries, her benign smile expressed the dignified restraint that usually accompanies the arrival of haute cuisine.

In retrospect, every design element at Schrafft's was calculated to allow middle-class patrons to believe that they had been enveloped by the same understated atmosphere ordinarily reserved for people of wealth. Little did I know then that I had experienced my first example of dining as theater, and that the experience had been superbly produced.

In common with design for the theater, restaurant design encompasses the journey from an abstract idea to a physical reality. Unlike the theater, though, where the playwright supplies the concrete framework (a script), the restaurateur and chef—often the acknowledged star of the production—ordinarily provide only a concept, accompanied by suggestions about the prospective mood and atmosphere of their project. Drawing on imagination and a hefty dose of research, the designer then sets out to transform their concept into a specific vision.

When I had the privilege of designing Nobu for Nobuyuki Matsuhisa, I understood from the get-go that I had to depict Nobu's genius for blending the finest foods and techniques of traditional Japanese cookery with those of the West, particularly South America. It was my job to create the visual equivalent of Nobu's highly sophisticated, minimalist culinary wonders.

No matter the final result, be it a fantasy world, a Jungian dream come to life, or a loving evocation of the past, the design must have the power to immerse diners into a world that is as unexpected as it is inimitable. Balthazar, Pastis, and Odeon plunge diners into worlds that suggest Belle Époque Parisian brasseries with enormous success. Michael Schulson's Buddakan is a monumental, cavernous space that evokes Broadway theatricality as much as it does Hollywood glamour, in a bold and surreal wonderland of over-the-top re-interpretations of Asian and French motifs.

Designers know that every space is inherently dramatic. When a restaurant occupies a space originally created for a diametrically different purpose, the element of surprise produces an especially dramatic result. A visit to Grand Central Terminal demonstrates that the cool modernism of Metrazur and the romantic scenography of Michael Jordan's The Steakhouse co-exist comfortably within the Beaux Arts masterpiece. On Museum Mile, Café Sabarsky resides in a landmarked mansion built in 1914 by Carrère & Hastings (the architects of the New York Public Library), which has housed some of the most famous of New York society over the last century. Now this space has been transformed into the Neue Galerie, a museum of early modern German and Austrian art, which also boasts this ode to the old-style Vienna café with dark wood walls, marble-topped tables, and reproductions of period objects housed within the museum. Head downtown and you will discover that the East Village people-watchers' hangout, B Bar and Grill (a.k.a. Bowery Bar) occupies a former gas station. Further south on the Bowery, Capitale, a part of New York City's portfolio of grander-than-grand dining rooms, makes its home in Stanford White's marbled and cavernous Bowery Savings Bank.

In his classic essay, "Here is New York," E. B. White chooses an old willow tree in Turtle Bay to symbolize life in our city. The tree represents "life under difficulties, growth against odds, sap rise in the midst of concrete and steady reaching for the sun." Those qualities are inherently dramatic, but then everything in New York is dramatic. Like the multitudes before me and the multitudes to come, New York City is my Emerald City. I feel honored to be a participant in our shared drama of astonishment.

AFTERWORD

DANNY MEYER

I am enormously proud to be a member of New York's hospitality community. It is world-class in every way.

I did not set out, initially, to parlay my political science degree into a career in the restaurant business. But because my father's business had to do with tourism in France and Italy, I grew up with the privilege of traveling, experiencing wonderful restaurants, and even working as a tour guide in Rome by the time I was twenty. I developed a passion for the hospitality business, for wanting to make people happy. I discovered that I was good at it. I believe it's in my genes. By the time I was twenty-seven, I had opened Union Square Cafe in Manhattan. There you have the seeds of my career.

There is probably no greater stage for a restaurateur than New York. As an adjunct to an art program, I opened a hot dog stand in the middle of Madison Square Park, and before I knew it the national press had noticed. There is a voracious audience for both food and news about food, and if you have something to add to the culinary dialogue, your story can reach the world just because this is New York. But along with the megaphone comes the microscope. In New York you might have a loyal following, but there are also people ready to pounce on your every foible. There is enormous competition and scrutiny, and these factors present a challenge. But they also raise the bar for excellence, and I have come to crave this dynamic atmosphere.

When a worthy competitor opens next door, of course it initially sends a shiver. But if your neighbor's business is good, it actually brings in new patrons for your restaurant and helps you maintain your edge. So many of our customers have become more sophisticated and demanding, which keeps our outlook fresh and vital. You cannot coast in New York.

Chefs were the trailblazers as professionals. They ratified the field for everyone. Now, along with restaurateurs and wine professionals, they have become entrepreneurs. When I started in this business, you did not have the fine-dining restaurant groups that exist and thrive today. Hospitality is a field in which anyone who works hard can rise. The profession has constantly welcomed and supported immigrant groups, and their success stories are legendary.

Although the competition is fierce, the New York restaurant community is also tightly knit and incredibly collegial, especially when compared with many other industries. We collaborate effectively on cause-related work as well as promotional events. We are there for each other.

Throughout the year, quietly and instinctively, restaurant professionals voluntarily do well by doing good. Scores of New York restaurants contribute to City Harvest, the organization that rescues leftover food and redirects it to where it is needed the most. Restaurants have generously provided leadership and talent to raise millions of dollars and to help Share Our Strength feed the needy, to help Citymeals-on-Wheels provide meals for the homebound elderly, and to help C-Cap to train inner-city students to become chefs and cooks. These efforts have helped to bond the members of the community, to bring people together.

I would go as far as to say that the fabric—not just the collective stomach—of New York has been nourished, nurtured, and enriched by this great industry.

But none of this would be possible without the continuing support of the restaurant-going public. By frequenting restaurants and treating them and their staffs with the same respect you expect them to shower on you at dinner, you also sustain the community. It's the best way to ensure that New York will maintain its position as the greatest restaurant city on the planet.

SOURCES

Not only is New York's restaurant landscape rich and diverse, it is matched by the markets that provide the ingredients necessary for preparing everything from a simple, top-notch broiled steak or a perfect Caesar salad, to glassy Korean noodles infused with soy sauce, tender okra needing an Indian spice cabinet, or a Mexican salsa made with the right blend of fresh and dried chiles. At one time, it took a trip to an ethnic neighborhood to find some of these exotic seasonings and vegetables. It still may be the case, but increasingly, a wide range of Asian, Hispanic, and Middle Eastern products are sold in the big food halls and even in supermarkets.

FOOD HALLS

The well-stocked food halls scattered throughout the city can be the one-stop shopping resource needed for most recipes. They sell packaged groceries, spices, and condiments as well as produce, meats, game, and seafood. Some, like Dean & DeLuca and Zabar's, have well-stocked housewares departments.

Agata & Valentina, 1505 First Avenue (79th Street), Manhattan, 212-452-0690; www.agatavalentina.com.

Amish Market, see www.amishfinefood.com.

Balducci's, 155 West 66th Street (Broadway), Manhattan, 212-653-8320; 81 Eighth Avenue (14th Street), Manhattan, 212-741-3700; www.suttongourmet.com.

A. L. Bazzini, 339 Greenwich Street (Jay Street), Manhattan, 212-334-1280; www.bazzininuts.com.

Chelsea Market, 75 Ninth Avenue (15th Street), Manhattan, 212-243-6005; www.chelseamarket.com.

Citarella, see www.citarella.com.

Dean & DeLuca, see www.deandeluca.com.

Eli's Manhattan and the Vinegar Factory, 1411 Third Avenue (80th Street), Manhattan, 212-717-8100; 431 East 91st Street (York Avenue), Manhattan, 212-987-0885; www.elizabar.com.

Fairway, see www.fairwaymarket.com.

Garden of Eden, see www.gardenofedengourmet.com.

Gourmet Garage, see www.gourmetgarage.com.

Grace's Marketplace, 1237 Third Avenue (71st Street), Manhattan, 212-737-0600; www.gracesmarketplace.com.

Todaro Bros., 555 Second Avenue (30th Street), Manhattan, 212-532-0633; www.todarobros.com.

Whole Foods, see www.wholefoodsmarket.com.

Zabar's, 2245 Broadway (80th Street), Manhattan, 212-787-2000; www.zabars.com.

ETHNIC MARKETS
Where the big, generalized food halls may fall short, certain ethnic markets take over to stock the pantry with exotic ingredients.

Bangkok Center Grocery, 104 Mosco Street (Mott Street), Manhattan, 212-732-8916; www.thai-grocery.com. *Asian*

Despaña Brand Foods, 408 Broome Street (Centre Street), Manhattan, 212-219-5050; 86-17 Northern Boulevard (86th Street), Queens, 718-779-4971; www.despanabrandfoods.com. *Spanish*

Foods of India, 121 Lexington Avenue (28th Street), Manhattan, 212-683-4419. *Indian*

Han Ah Reum Market, 25 West 32nd Street, Manhattan, 212-695-3283; 29-02 Union Street, Queens, 718-445-5656. *Korean*

Hong Kong Supermarket, 109 East Broadway (Pike Street), Manhattan, 212-227-3388; 6013 Eighth Avenue (60th Street), Brooklyn, 718-438-2288; 82-02 45th Avenue (Broadway), Queens, 718-651-3838; 37-11 Main Street (37th Avenue), Queens, 718-539-6868; 5672 49th Place (Maspeth Avenue), Queens, 718-821-9888. *Chinese*

Kalustyan's, 123 Lexington Avenue (28th Street), Manhattan, 212-685-3451; www.kalustyans.com. *Middle Eastern, Indian*

Kam Man, 200 Canal Street (Mott Street), Manhattan, 212-571-0330. *Chinese*

Katagiri, 224 East 59th Street (Second Avenue), Manhattan, 212-755-3566; www.katagiri.com. *Japanese*

M2M, 200 East 11th Street (Third Avenue), Manhattan, 212-353-2698; 2935 Broadway (West 115th Street), Manhattan, 212-280-4600. *Japanese*

Pacific Supermarket, 75-01 Broadway (75th Street), Queens, 718-507-8181. *Asian*

Patel Brothers, 37-27 74th Street (Northern Boulevard), Queens, 718-898-3445; 42-79C and 42-92 Main Street (Cherry Avenue), Queens, 718-661-1112; www.patelbrothersusa.com. *Indian*

Sahadi's, 187 Atlantic Avenue (Court Street), Brooklyn, 718-624-4550; www.sahadis.com. *Middle Eastern*

Sunrise Mart, 4 Stuyvesant Street (Ninth Street and Third Avenue), Manhattan, 212-598-3040; 494 Broome Street (Wooster Street), Manhattan, 212-279-0033. *Japanese*

HERBS AND SPICES
There are some markets that specialize in spices, seasonings, and condiments from every corner of the planet. *See also Ethnic Markets.*

Adriana's Caravan, www.adrianascaravan.com.

Aphrodisia, 264 Bleecker Street (Seventh Avenue), Manhattan, 212-989-6440.

Penzey's Spices, Grand Central Market, Lexington Avenue and 43rd Street, Manhattan, 212-972-2777; www.penzeys.com.

PRODUCE

Locally grown, seasonal produce is the stock-in-trade of the Greenmarket system, which has been in business since 1977. Farmers, cheese makers, fishermen, bakers, and other artisanal food producers from the surrounding region bring their products to sell on a regular schedule to all five boroughs, some throughout the year, others on a more limited basis. The Union Square Greenmarket, open on Mondays, Wednesdays, Fridays, and Saturdays, is the flagship. Information and schedules are available from 212-788-7476, www.cenyc.org. *See also Food Halls, Ethnic Markets.*

Greenwich Produce, Grand Central Market, Lexington Avenue and 43rd Street, Manhattan, 212-490-4444.

Manhattan Fruit Exchange, Chelsea Market, 75 Ninth Avenue (15th Street), Manhattan, 212-989-2444; www.chelseamarket.com.

SEAFOOD, MEAT, POULTRY, AND GAME

Most of the food halls have well-stocked seafood, meat, and poultry departments, but there are also many specialty stores.

SEAFOOD

Pisacane Midtown, 940 First Avenue (51st Street), Manhattan, 212-752-7560.

Randazzo's Seafood, 2327 Arthur Avenue (187th Street), Bronx, 718-367-4139.

Sea Breeze, 541 Ninth Avenue (40th Street), Manhattan, 212-563-7537; 8500 18th Avenue (85th Street), Brooklyn, 718-259-9693.

Tan My My, 249 Grand Street (Chrystie Street), Manhattan, 212-966-7878.

Wild Edibles, Grand Central Market, Lexington Avenue and 43rd Street, Manhattan, 212-687-4255; 535 Third Avenue (35th Street), Manhattan, 212-213-8552; www.wildedibles.com.

MEAT, POULTRY, AND GAME

D'Artagnan, www.dartagnan.com.

DeBragga and Spitler, www.debragga.com.

Faicco's Pork Store, 260 Bleecker Street (Seventh Avenue), Manhattan, 212-243-1974; 6511 11th Avenue, Brooklyn, 718-236-0119.

Koglin Royal Hams, 303 Grand Street (Allen Street), Manhattan, 212-499-0725; www.koglinroyalhams.com.

Lobel's Prime Meats, 1096 Madison Avenue (82nd Street), Manhattan, 212-737-1372, 800-556-2357; www.lobels.com.

Schaller & Weber, 1654 Second Avenue (86th Street), Manhattan, 212-879-3047, 800-847-4115; www.schallerweber.com.

MUSHROOMS AND TRUFFLES

For fresh white and black truffles, and also for mushroom products, prices are sometimes a trifle lower at specialty wholesale-retail markets than in the food halls.

Truffette, 104 Avenue B (Seventh Street), Manhattan, 212-505-5813; www.sos-chefs.com.

PASTA

A few pasta-makers have been in business for generations.

Borgatti's Ravioli, 632 East 187th Street (Hughes Avenue), Bronx, 718-367-3799; www.borgattis.com.

Raffetto's, 144 West Houston Street (Sullivan Street), Manhattan, 212-777-1261.

CHEESE

Some of the best cheese assortments are sold at markets like Fairway, Zabar's, and Dean & DeLuca. In addition, there are several excellent cheese purveyors in the city.

Artisanal, 2 Park Avenue (32nd Street), Manhattan, 212-532-4033; www.artisanalbistro.com.

DiPalo Fine Foods, 200 Grand Street (Mott Street), Manhattan, 212-226-1033.

Formaggio Essex, Essex Market, 120 Essex Street (Delancey Street), Manhattan, 212-982-8200; www.formaggioessex.com.

Murray's Cheese Shop, 245 Bleecker Street (Sixth Avenue), Manhattan, 212-243-3289; Grand Central Market, Lexington Avenue and 43rd Street, Manhattan, 212-922-1540; also 888-692-4339; www.murrayscheese.com.

Saxelby Cheesemonger, Essex Market, 120 Essex Street (Delancey Street), Manhattan, 212-228-8204; www.saxelbycheese.com.

COOKWARE

A number of shops have well-edited cookware inventories.

A Cook's Companion, 197 Atlantic Avenue (Court Street), Brooklyn, 718-852-6901.

The Art of Cooking, www.artofcookingnyc.com.

Bowery Kitchen Restaurant Equipment & Supplies, Chelsea Market, 75 Ninth Avenue (15th Street), Manhattan, 212-376-4982; www.bowerykitchens.com.

Broadway Panhandler, 65 East Eighth Street (Broadway), Manhattan, 212-966-3434, 866-266-5927; www.broadwaypanhandler.com.

Dean & DeLuca, see Food Halls.

Gracious Home, see www.gracioushome.com.

New York Cake and Bake Distributors, 56 West 22nd Street (Sixth Avenue), Manhattan, 212-675-2253, 800-942-2539.

Sur la Table, 75 Spring Street (Crosby Street), Manhattan, 212-966-3375; www.surlatable.com.

Twin Supply Inc., 1201 Castleton Avenue (Roe Street), Staten Island, 718-442-1010; www.twinsupply.com.

Williams-Sonoma, see www.williams-sonoma.com.

Zabar's, see Food Halls.

WINE AND LIQUOR

Every neighborhood has wine shops and, given the worldwide selection that lines their shelves, it is hard NOT to find an acceptable wine for dinner. Here are some of the more outstanding examples.

Acker Merrall & Condit Co., 160 West 72nd Street (Amsterdam Avenue), Manhattan, 212-787-1700; www.ackerwines.com.

Astor Wines & Spirits, 399 Lafayette (East Fourth Street), Manhattan, 212-674-7500; www.astorwines.com.

Best Cellars, 1291 Lexington Avenue (87th Street), Manhattan, 212-426-4200; 2246 Broadway (80th Street), Manhattan, 212-362-8730; www.bestcellars.com.

Bierkraft, 191 Fifth Avenue (Berkeley Place), Brooklyn, 718-230-7600; www.bierkraft.com.

Burgundy Wine Co., 143 West 26th Street (Seventh Avenue), Manhattan, 212-691-9092; www.burgundywinecompany.com.

Chambers St. Wines, 148 Chambers Street (Greenwich Street), Manhattan, 212-227-1434; www.chambersstwines.com.

Italian Wine Merchants, 108 East 16th Street (Park Avenue), Manhattan, 212-473-2323; www.italianwinemerchant.com.

Morrell & Co., 1 Rockefeller Plaza (49th Street), Manhattan, 212-688-9370, 800-969-4637; www.morrellwine.com.

Park Avenue Liquor Shop, 292 Madison Avenue (40th Street), Manhattan, 212-685-2442; www.parkaveliquor.com.

PJ Liquor Warehouse, 4898 Broadway (204th Street), Manhattan, 212-567-5500; www.pjwine.com.

Red White & Bubbly, 211 Fifth Avenue (Union Street), Brooklyn, 718-636-9463; www.redwhiteandbubbly.com.

Sherry-Lehmann, 505 Park Avenue (59th Street), Manhattan, 212-838-7500; www.sherry-lehmann.com.

Skyview Discount Wines & Liquors, 5681 Riverdale Avenue (259th Street), Bronx, 718-601-8222, also 888-759-8466; www.skyviewwine.com.

BIBLIOGRAPHY

Many of the restaurants and chefs included in this book have cookbooks of their own, which are worth consulting for more recipes and background. Some have more than one book, but only the most recently published book has been listed.

ADOUR
Ducasse, Alain. *Grand Livre de Cuisine*. New York: Stewart, Tabori & Chang, 2007.

ANTONUCCI
Antonucci, Francesco and Adam Tihany. *Venetian Taste*. Text by Florence Fabricant. New York: Abbeville Press, 1994.

AQUAVIT
Samuelsson, Marcus. *The Soul of a New Cuisine*. New York: Wiley, 2006.

ARTISANAL
Brennan, Terrance, and Andrew Friedman. *Artisanal Cooking*. New York: Wiley, 2005.

AUREOLE
Palmer, Charlie. *The Practical Guide to the New American Kitchen*. New York: Melcher Media, 2006.

BABBO
Batali, Mario. *Italian Grill*. New York: Ecco, 2008.

BALDORIA
Pellegrino, Frank. *Rao's Recipes from the Neighborhood*. New York: St. Martin's Press, 2004.

BALTHAZAR
McNally, Keith, and Riad Nasr, Lee Hanson, and Kathryn Kellinger. *The Balthazar Cookbook*. New York: Clarkson N. Potter, 2003.

BAR AMERICAIN
Flay, Bobby, with Stephanie Banyas, and Sally Jackson. *Bobby Flay's Grill It!* New York: Clarkson N. Potter, 2008.

BEACON
Malouf, Waldy, and Melissa Clark. *High Heat*. New York: Broadway Books, 2003.

BOULEY
Bouley, David, Mario Lohninger, and Melissa Clark. *East of Paris*. Hopewell, New Jersey: Ecco, 2003.

CAFÉ DES ARTISTES
Ferretti, Fred. *Café des Artistes*. New York: Lebhar-Friedman, 2000.

CENTOLIRE
Luongo, Pino and Mark Strausman. *Two Meatballs in the Italian Kitchen*. New York: Artisan, 2007.

CHANTERELLE
Waltuck, David, and Andrew Friedman.
Chanterelle. Newtown, Conn.: Taunton, 2008.

CITY BAKERY
Rubin, Maury. *Book of Tarts*. New York:
William Morrow, 1995.

CONVIVIO
White, Michael. *Fiamma: The Essence of
Contemporary Italian Cooking*. New York:
Wiley, 2006.

CRAFT
Colicchio, Tom. *Craft of Cooking*. New York:
Clarkson N. Potter, 2003.

DANIEL
Boulud, Daniel, and Melissa Clark. *Braise*.
New York: Ecco, 2006.

DÉVI
Saran, Suvir, with Raquel Pelzel. *American
Masala*. New York: Clarkson N. Potter, 2007.

DO HWA
Kwak, Jenny, and Liz Fried. *Dok Suni*. New
York: St. Martin's Press, 1998.

FELIDIA
Bastianich, Lidia. *Lidia's Italy*. New York:
Knopf, 2007.

FIAMMA
Trabocchi, Fabio. *Cucina of Le Marche*.
New York: Ecco, 2006.

THE FOUR SEASONS
Mariani, John, with Alex Von Bidder.
The Four Seasons. New York: Crown, 1994.

FRESCO BY SCOTTO
Scotto Family. *Italian Comfort Food*.
New York: Ecco, 2005.

GOTHAM BAR & GRILL
Portale, Alfred. *Alfred Portale Simple
Pleasures*. New York: William Morrow
Cookbooks, 2004.

HARRY CIPRIANI
Cipriani, Arrigo. *The Harry's Bar Cookbook*.
London: John Blake Publishing, Ltd., 2006.

HILL COUNTRY
Karmel, Elizabeth. *Taming the Flame*. New
York: Wiley, 2005.

JEAN GEORGES
Vongerichten, Jean-Georges. *Asian Flavors of
Jean-Georges*. New York: Broadway Books,
2007.

LE BERNARDIN
Ripert, Eric, and Christine Muhlke. *On the
Line*. New York: Artisan, 2008.

LE CIRQUE
Maccioni, Egi, and Peter Kaminsky. *The
Maccioni Family Cookbook*. New York:
Stewart, Tabori & Chang, 2003.

MAYA
Sandoval, Richard, David Ricketts, and Ignacio Urquiza. *Modern Mexican Flavors.* New York: Stewart, Tabori & Chang, 2002.

MAZE
Ramsay, Gordon. *Gordon Ramsay's Three Star Chef.* Toronto, Ontario: Key Porter Books, 2008.

MOLYVOS
Botsacos, Jim, and Judith Choate. *The New Greek Cuisine.* New York: Broadway Books, 2006.

MORIMOTO
Morimoto, Masuharu. *Morimoto.* New York: DK Publishing, 2007.

NOBU
Matsuhisa, Nobuyuki. *Nobu: The Cookbook.* Translated by Laura Holland. New York: Kodansha International, 2001.

OLIVES
English, Todd, Paige Retus, and Sally Sampson. *The Olives Dessert Table.* New York: Simon & Schuster, 2000.

OUEST
Valenti, Tom, and Andrew Friedman. *Soups, Stews, and One-Pot Meals.* New York: Scribner, 2003.

OYSTER BAR
Grand Central Oyster Bar Restaurant and Sandy Ingber. *The Grand Central Oyster Bar and Restaurant Complete Seafood Cookbook.* New York: Stewart, Tabori & Chang, 1999.

PALM
Binns, Brigit Legere. *Pizza: And Other Savory Pies.* New York: Fireside, 2008.

PATSY'S
Scognamillo, Sal, and Nancy Sinatra. *Patsy's Cookbook.* New York: Clarkson N. Potter, 2002.

PAYARD BISTRO
Payard, François, and Anne E. McBride. *Chocolate Epiphany.* New York: Clarkson N. Potter, 2008.

PEARL OYSTER BAR
Charles, Rebecca, and Deborah Di Clementi. *Lobster Rolls and Blueberry Pie.* New York: Regan Books, 2003.

PER SE
Keller, Thomas. *Under Pressure: Cooking Sous Vide.* New York: Artisan, 2008.

PORTER HOUSE NY
Lomonaco, Michael. *Nightly Specials.* New York: William Morrow Cookbooks, 2004.

RED CAT
Bradley, Jimmy, and Andrew Friedman. *The Red Cat Cookbook*. New York: Clarkson N. Potter, 2006.

RIVER CAFÉ
DeLissio, Joseph. *The River Cafe Wine Primer*. Boston: Little, Brown and Company, 2000.

ROSA MEXICANO
Santibanez, Roberto, and Christopher Styler. *Rosa's New Mexican Table*. New York: Artisan, 2007.

ROY'S NEW YORK
Yamaguchi, Roy, with John Harrisson. *Roy's Fish & Seafood*. Berkeley: Ten Speed Press, 2005.

SARDI'S
Sardi, Vincent, and George Shea. *Sardi's Bar Guide*. New York: Ballantine Books, 1992.

SCARPETTA
Conant, Scott, and Joanne McAllister Smart. *Bold Italian*. New York: Broadway Books, 2008.

SD26 NY
May, Tony. *Italian Cuisine*. New York: St. Martin's Press, 2005.

SECOND AVENUE DELI
Lebewohl, Sharon and Jack, Rena Bulkin. *The 2nd Avenue Deli Cookbook*. New York: Villard, 1999.

TAVERN ON THE GREEN
LeRoy, Kay, and Jennifer Oz LeRoy. *Tavern on the Green*. New York: Artisan, 2009.

TELEPAN
Telepan, Bill, and Andrew Friedman. *Inspired by Ingredients*. New York: Simon & Schuster, 2004.

TOWN
Zakarian, Geoffrey, with David Gibbons. *Geoffrey Zakarian's Town / Country*. New York: Clarkson N. Potter, 2006.

'21' CLUB
Lomonaco, Michael, with Donna Forsman. *The '21' Cookbook*. New York: Doubleday, 1995.

ACKNOWLEDGMENTS

This is the second time I have collaborated on a cookbook with my daughter, Patricia Fabricant, a gifted graphic designer. Working with her is always a pleasure. It was largely thanks to her that the job of writing this book landed in my lap. Thanks also to Brad Fazzari and Joshua Somers at NYC & Company for their help with this revised edition. At Rizzoli, Charles Miers, Christopher Steighner, and Jono Jarrett cracked the whip when I doubted that the deadlines could be met, and somehow, it all came together in record time.

Special thanks also go to Sylvie Bigar, recipe tester par excellence, for her enthusiasm and talent in the kitchen.

—FLORENCE FABRICANT

We would like to acknowledge the following key individuals for their support: Phillip Baltz, Jane Dystel, Scott Feldman, George Fertitta, Frank Giallorenzo, Anthony Giglio, Evan Korn, Buzzy O'Keeffe, Emily Rafferty, Sheryl Shade, Jeffrey Stewart, Commissioner Iris Weinshall, Clark Wolf, Keith Yazmir, Melanie Young, and Jenny Zinman.

A special thank you to the NYC & Company restaurant committee and book contributors who enthusiastically provided their insight about New York City dining.

Lastly, we extend our appreciation and gratitude to the participating restaurants that have made this endeavor possible.

—NYC & COMPANY

INDEX OF RESTAURANTS

Convivio (78)
45 Tudor City Place
212-599-5045

Corton (210)
239 West Broadway
212-219-2777

Craft (72)
43 East 19th Street
212-780-0880

Daniel (178)
60 East 65th Street
212-288-0033

Dévi (106)
8 East 18th Street
212-691-1300

Do Hwa (34)
55 Carmine Street
212-414-1224

Estiatorio Milos (123)
125 West 55th Street
212-245-7400

Fairway Steakhouse (198)
2127 Broadway, 2nd Floor
212-595-1888

Felidia (86)
243 East 58th Street
212-758-1479

Fiamma (84)
206 Spring Street
212-653-0100

Fig & Olive (21)
Uptown
808 Lexington Avenue
212-207-4555
Midtown
10 East 52nd Street
212-319-2002
Downtown
420 West 13th Street
212-924-1200

Firebird (197)
365 West 46th Street
212-586-0244

Fleur de Sel (142)
5 East 20th Street
212-460-9100

The Four Seasons (156)
99 East 52nd Street
212-754-9494

Fresco by Scotto (83)
34 East 52nd Street
212-935-3434

Gotham Bar & Grill (66)
12 East 12th Street
212-620-4020

The Grocery (46)
288 Smith Street
(Brooklyn)
718-596-3335

Hangawi (89)
12 East 32nd Street
212-213-0077

Harry's Cafe (152)
One Hanover Square
212-785-9200

Harry Cipriani (241)
Sherry-Netherland Hotel
781 Fifth Avenue
212-753-5566

Hill Country (196)
30 West 26th Street
212-255-4544

I Trulli (100)
122 East 27th Street
212-481-7372

Jean Georges (30)
Trump International Hotel
1 Central Park West
212-299-3900

Jewel Bako (27)
239 East 5th Street
212-979-1012

Kai (215)
Ito En
822 Madison Avenue
212-988-7277

La Goulue (44)
746 Madison Avenue
212-988-8169

L'Absinthe (33)
227 East 67th Street
212-794-4950

Le Bernardin (132)
155 West 51st Street
212-554-1515

Le Cirque (208)
One Beacon Court
151 East 58th Street
212-303-7788

Le Colonial (74)
149 East 57th Street
212-752-0808

Le Pain Quotidien (113)
100 Grand Street
212-625-9009
1131 Madison Avenue
212-327-4900
1336 First Avenue
212-717-4800
833 Lexington Avenue
212-755-5810
50 West 72nd Street
212-712-9700
38 East 19th Street
212-673-7900
for other locations, see
www.painquotidien.com

Le Périgord (164)
405 East 52nd Street
212-755-6244

Lunetta (228)
920 Broadway
212-533-3663
116 Smith Street
(Brooklyn)
718-488-6269

Mario's (82)
2342 Arthur Avenue
718-584-1188 (Bronx)

Marseille (160)
630 Ninth Avenue
212-333-2323

Maya (222)
1191 First Avenue
212-585-1818

Maze by Gordon
Ramsay (150)
151 West 54th Street
212-468-8889

Michael's (99)
24 West 55th Street
212-767-0555

Molyvos (236)
871 Seventh Avenue
212-582-7500

Momofuku (246)
207 Second Avenue
212-254-3500

Morimoto (124)
88 Tenth Avenue
212-989-8883

Nam (205)
110 Reade Street
212-267-1777

Nobu (128)
105 Hudson Street
212-219-0500

Olives (60)
W Union Square Hotel
201 Park Avenue South
212-353-8345

One If by Land,
Two If by Sea (220)
17 Barrow Street
212-228-0822

Ouest (28)
2315 Broadway
212-580-8700

Oyster Bar (59)
Grand Central Terminal
212-490-6650

Palm (71)
837 Second Avenue
212-687-2953

Pampano (40)
209 East 49th Street
212-751-4545

Patsy's (138)
236 West 56th Street
212-247-3491

Payard Bistro (218)
1032 Lexington Avenue
212-717-5252

Pearl Oyster Bar (110)
18 Cornelia Street
212-691-8211

Per Se (136)
Time Warner Center
10 Columbus Circle, 4th Floor
212-823-9349

Peter Luger Steak House
(192)
178 Broadway
718-387-7400 (Brooklyn)

Petrossian (94)
182 West 58th Street
212-245-2214

Porter House New York (36)
Time Warner Center
10 Columbus Circle, 4th Floor
212-823-9474

Red Cat (200)
227 Tenth Avenue
212-242-1122

Relish (68)
225 Wythe Avenue
718-963-4546 (Brooklyn)

River Café (118)
1 Water Street
718-522-5200 (Brooklyn)

Rosa Mexicano (162)
61 Columbus Avenue
212-977-7700
1063 First Avenue
212-753-7407

Roy's New York (120)
Marriott Financial Center
130 Washington Street
212-266-6262

Sapori D'Ischia (102)
55-13 37th Avenue
718-446-1500 (Queens)

Sardi's (243)
234 West 44th Street
212-221-8440

Savoy (203)
70 Prince Street
212-219-8570

Scarpetta (166)
355 West 14th Street
212-691-0555

SD26 NY (176)
19 East 26th Street
212-265-5959

Second Avenue Deli (52)
162 East 33rd Street
212-689-9000

Shun Lee Palace (181)
155 East 55th Street
212-371-8844

Smith & Wollensky (184)
797 Third Avenue
212-753-1530

Strip House (194)
13 East 12th Street
212-328-0000

Tamarind (204)
41-43 East 22nd Street
212-674-7400

Taste (226)
1413 Third Avenue
212-717-9798

Tavern on the Green (64)
Central Park West at
67th Street
212-873-3200

T-Bar Steak and Lounge
(232)
1278 Third Avenue
212-772-0404

Telepan (54)
72 West 69th Street
212-580-4300

Tocqueville (212)
1 East 15th Street
212-647-1515

Town (50)
Chambers Hotel
15 West 56th Street
212-582-4445

Trattoria dell'Arte (108)
900 Seventh Avenue
212-245-9800

'21' Club (38)
21 West 52nd Street
212-582-7200

Union Square Cafe (116)
21 East 16th Street
212-243-4020

Veritas (230)
43 East 20th Street
212-353-3700

Wallsé (172)
344 West 11th Street
212-352-2300

Waverly Inn (148)
16 Bank Street
212-929-4377

wd50 (224)
50 Clinton Street
212-477-2900

Zarela (146)
953 Second Avenue
212-644-6740

INDEX OF RESTAURANTS BY LOCATION

UPPER EAST SIDE
Antonucci
Aureole
Centolire
Daniel
Fig & Olive
Harry Cipriani
Kai
La Goulue
L'Absinthe
Le Pain Quotidien
Maya
Payard Bistro
Taste

UPPER WEST SIDE
Café des Artistes
Calle Ocho
Fairway Steakhouse
Jean Georges
Le Pain Quotidien
Ouest
Per Se
Porter House NY
Rosa Mexicano
Tavern on the Green
Telepan

BROOKLYN
Al Di La
The Grocery
Lunetta
Peter Luger Steak House
Relish
River Café

BRONX
Mario's

QUEENS
Sapori D'Ischia

STATEN ISLAND
Angelina's

INDEX

CONVERSION CHART

All conversions are approximate.

LIQUID CONVERSIONS

U.S.	METRIC
1 tsp	5 ml
1 tbs	15 ml
2 tbs	30 ml
3 tbs	45 ml
¼ cup	60 ml
⅓ cup	75 ml
⅓ cup + 1 tbs	90 ml
⅓ cup + 2 tbs	100 ml
½ cup	120 ml
⅔ cup	150 ml
¾ cup	180 ml
¾ cup + 2 tbs	200 ml
1 cup	240 ml
1 cup + 2 tbs	275 ml
1¼ cups	300 ml
1⅓ cups	325 ml
1½ cups	350 ml
1⅔ cups	375 ml
1¾ cups	400 ml
1¾ cups + 2 tbs	450 ml
2 cups (1 pint)	475 ml
2½ cups	600 ml
3 cups	720 ml
4 cups (1 quart)	945 ml (1,000 ml is 1 liter)

WEIGHT CONVERSIONS

U.S./U.K.	METRIC
½ oz	14 g
1 oz	28 g
1½ oz	43 g
2 oz	57 g
2½ oz	71 g
3 oz	85 g
3½ oz	100 g
4 oz	113 g
5 oz	142 g
6 oz	170 g
7 oz	200 g
8 oz	227 g
9 oz	255 g
10 oz	284 g
11 oz	312 g
12 oz	340 g
13 oz	368 g
14 oz	400 g
15 oz	425 g
1 lb	454 g

OVEN TEMPERATURES

°F	GAS MARK	°C
250	½	120
275	1	140
300	2	150
325	3	165
350	4	180
375	5	190
400	6	200
425	7	220
450	8	230
475	9	240
500	10	260
550	Broil	290

PHOTOGRAPHY CREDITS

Quentin Bacon: 227; Bruce Buck/Rockwell Group: 1, 24; Ben Fink: 106; Jean-Pierre Gabriel: 112, 113; Richard Gilbert: 202; Stefano Giovanni: 142; Gayle Gleason: 42; Mick Hales: 235; Anne Hall: 180; Fransisco Herrera: 107; Michelle Hood: 95; Warren Jager: 236; Sean Johnson: 50, 80, 92; David Joseph: 124, 125; Noah Kalina: 229, 246, 247; Bruce Katz/ Rockwell Group: 163; Michael Katz: 23; L'Absinthe: 33; Photo by Lanteck Studios: 34; John Lei: 167; Le Perigord: 164; Beckett Logan: 109; © Peter Medilek / ClausNY: 5, 23, 58, 70, 79, 102, 138, 144, 198; Michael Mundy: 74; Fumiko Nozawa: 220; Robert Polidori: 225; © Paul Raeside: 150; © Liz Steger, www.lizsteger.com: 157, 185, 219; Steph Graphics: 126; Buff Strickland: 26, 111; Joseph Tabacca: 40; Michael Tong: 180; '21' Club: 39; Paul Warchol/ Rockwell Group: 129, 195, 253.